Rising to the challenge of ma
and equitable will hinge on ou.
eration of graduates with the tools and the capabilities they
need – as well as inspiring them around the many possibilities.
Reorienting management education towards those goals will be
vital. This book is an important contribution in that direction.

A persuasive account, packed with novel and interesting
ideas, on how management education can further play its part
in equipping the next generation of graduates with the skills,
capabilities and – importantly – the confidence they need to
meet our ever-growing sustainability challenge.

Paul Polman, CEO, Unilever

This book will excite a lot of people. For some, it's about putting
business in wider context; for others, a rich source of advice on
the future of management education; for still others, a call to
lead from wherever you are in redefining how we do business.
100 strong ideas that together form a new map of critical thinking in the world of action.

**Rich Lyons, Dean, Haas School of Business, University
of California Berkeley**

Giselle Weybrecht's innovative and inspiring book is an excel-
lent example of the practical application of concrete and sharp
ideas on how to advance the sustainability agenda within business programmes. Redefining the purpose of business education and shifting its paradigm towards developing effective,
efficient, and, foremost, socially responsible managers is of
paramount importance. *The Future MBA: 100 Ideas for Making
Sustainability the Business of Business Education* is a commend-
able blueprint for tomorrow's management education and an
extremely enjoyable read.

Eric Cornuel, Director General & CEO, EFMD

Giselle Weybrecht's new book is like a great brainstorming session: the good, provocative, ideas just keep coming. As a whole, the collection of short essays provides a comprehensive, holistic checklist for reinventing a graduate business education that can create positive social and environmental impact.

Eban Goodstein, Director, Bard MBA in Sustainability

The Future MBA offers inspiring, yet practical, ideas to develop the responsible leaders of tomorrow. It is a must-read for all PRME signatories looking to transform management education, research and thought leadership globally, as well as any individual who is interested in contemplating the business degree of the future and gleaning inspiration for how we might make it a reality.

Jonas Haertle, Head, PRME Secretariat, UN Global Compact Office

Giselle Weybrecht's *The Future MBA: 100 Ideas for Making Sustainability the Business of Business Education* is one of the most interesting professional books I have read in a long time, and hugely enjoyable. The vast majority of authors take as a given the institutional and regulatory constraints within which business schools have been operating, some for over a century. Refreshingly, Weybrecht sees business schools as potential change agents for a better world. Weybrecht's new book is of interest not only to the business school community, but will be an eye-opener to many officials in government and international development agencies, who may discover new allies in their efforts to attain the UN's Sustainable Development Goals.

Guy Pfeffermann, CEO, Global Business School Network

If we want to change how business is done, we need to think about how business is taught. *The Future MBA* envisions new approaches to business school curriculum and culture aimed at preparing students to be resilient and thoughtful sustainability leaders. Full of practical ideas that can be implemented by students and educators alike.

Katie Kross, Managing Director, Center for Energy, Development, and the Global Environment, Fuqua School of Business, Duke University

The Future MBA: 100 Ideas for Making Sustainability the Business of Business Education brings together creative and inspirational thoughts and ideas and also offering us a perspective of an MBA programme to create the leaders that our world needs – "capable of changing business for the good of all".

I strongly recommend this book to deans and directors of business schools, professors, experts at ranking institutions, policy-makers, and particularly to all students and candidates as it offers immense help in selecting an MBA, doctorate programme, or any management or leadership development programme.

Danica Purg, President, CEEMAN and IEDC Bled School of Management

In *The Future MBA* Ms Weybrecht redefines the boundaries of what is possible in business education, helping us to think beyond the long-standing customs and traditions of higher education. Read it and you'll come away believing, as I do, that business schools will not only change to survive, they will innovate to become vital engines of sustainable business and global prosperity.

Dan LeClair, Executive Vice President and Chief Strategy and Innovation Officer, AACSB

Giselle Weybrecht's new book provides us with insights and ideas that will shape management education for many years to come. It's a blueprint for successful business schools in the 21st century.

Professor Dipak C. Jain, Director, Sasin Graduate Institute of Business Administration, Chulalongkorn University

As evidenced by the 2015 Paris climate talks, UN SDGs, EU Circular Economy strategy and more, it is clear that the global sustainable development agenda has reached a vital crossroads. Giselle Weybrecht's new publication is perfectly timed, in that she reminds us of an uncontestable truth: that in order to advance prospects for a more sustainable world, systemic change and innovation are urgently needed in business education, so that the passion, mindsets, skills and talents of the next generation of leaders are more effectively harnessed and developed. Her book challenges and intrigues in equal measure, such that any reader will surely embrace a number of her key ideas – and hopefully inspire new ways of thinking and doing among business school peers and colleagues.

Simon Pickard, Director, International Programmes, ABIS – The Academy of Business in Society

The Future MBA

100 Ideas for Making Sustainability the
Business of Business Education

GISELLE WEYBRECHT

The Future
MBA

Greenleaf
PUBLISHING

© 2016 Greenleaf Publishing Limited

Published by Greenleaf Publishing Limited
Salts Mill, Victoria Road, Saltaire, BD18 3LA, UK
www.greenleaf-publishing.com

The right of Giselle Weybrecht to be identified as Author of this Work has
been asserted by her in accordance with sections 77 and 78 of the Copyright,
Designs and Patents Act 1988.

Cover by Sadie Gornall-Jones

Printed and bound by Printondemand-worldwide.com, UK

British Library Cataloguing in Publication Data:
    A catalogue record for this book is available from the British Library.

    ISBN-13: 978-1-78353-398-5 [hardback]
    ISBN-13: 978-1-78353-565-1 [paperback]
    ISBN-13: 978-1-78353-402-9 [PDF ebook]
    ISBN-13: 978-1-78353-566-8 [ePub ebook]

For Luca and Chloé
who should be able to grow up in a world where
sustainability is everybody's business

Contents

Acknowledgements

A big thank you to all those who supported, followed and promoted the original 100 ideas when they came out, in particular the dozens of champions at schools around the world who contacted me to say they were inspired by or even created new programmes based on some of these ideas. Thank you to my husband, Rich, my father, Earl, and friends and colleagues, who are always on hand to re-read my ideas. I hope that this book inspires at least one new idea that you can take with you, implement, and bring about the change that is needed.

Introduction

What is this book all about?

In mid-2014 I launched "Future MBA", 100 ideas posted online over 100 days, as an exploration of what the future business degree programme could look like – one that shapes the kind of leader that the planet and society needs. Rather than a specific roadmap, it was meant to be a source of inspiration. Some ideas could be put into practice tomorrow, some would require a complete rethinking of the way we view business education, and others were meant to encourage more ideas ... and more action to turn management education into a key player in moving the sustainability agenda forward.

Each idea brings with it multiple potential benefits, for the school, the students and, in particular, sustainability in its broadest sense. This book is based on those ideas.

Why did it come about?

When we talk about sustainability, we don't usually talk about the potential of business students and graduates in making that vision a reality. In fact, business graduates are often thought of as being a part of the problem rather than the solution. But every year hundreds of thousands of students graduate from business schools around the world and each and every one of them has the opportunity to influence what our future will look like. What if they all not only understood the core concepts related to sustainability but, more importantly, knew how to put those concepts into practice in ways that benefit their organizations, society and the planet? What if business schools were a crucial and indispensable part of creating a more sustainable society for all?

Unfortunately, the business school of today is not yet equipped or positioned to play that role. How do we take a moment to stand back and look at the bigger picture, and question the assumptions about what a business school looks like? What would the business school of the future look like? What should it look like? What do we need it to look like? How could we change it so that it formed and shaped the business leaders that our organizations and the planet need for a sustainable future, while at the same time creating a much deeper, more meaningful educational and life experience for the students themselves?

While the MBA was the initial inspiration for these 100 ideas, they are equally applicable to any business-related degree or in-house business-training programme. Most, if not all, can also be explored within non-business degrees.

How can I use this book?

Exciting changes in management education are coming from institutions of all shapes and sizes around the world. But the change process has only just begun. This book can be used as inspiration as you explore how to strengthen your educational institutions, plan the kinds of programmes you wish to start, think about how to differentiate and innovate existing programmes and how to create stronger business leaders. Use this book as inspiration to explore your own ideas or be inspired by them and make them your own.

Give copies to your staff, faculty, students and business and community partners in order to start a discussion together about how we can move forward. Even if you think, at first glance, that you are already implementing an idea, explore how you can push it further, strengthen it, and build upon it. Think an idea isn't possible? Then use it as a starting point to determine how it may be possible and how to make it possible, because, really, anything is.

This is where you start.

Looking ahead

How could business education be transformed to better prepare the kinds of sustainability leaders our businesses and our planet need? At the end of the original 100 days, I sat down, surrounded by all of the ideas, to see what kind of an MBA they had created. Here is the result of that effort before exploring the ideas themselves.

1. It will focus on developing the individual

We, as individuals, have more power than we realize. Businesses are made up of individuals, many of whom are business graduates, making decisions on a day-to-day basis that affect their businesses and the world around them. The future business school isn't just about developing more sustainability leaders; it is about forming individuals who have both a better understanding of the world around them, how they fit within that world, and their responsibilities towards it. This will lead to better decision-making, taking into account the needs of business, people and the planet. It is ultimately about creating graduates capable of changing business for the good of all.

2. It will embed sustainability seamlessly

Sustainability should be taught based on what is currently happening in the business world, and what we need and would like to see happen in the world. Presenting sustainability as a separate concept is not useful to the majority of students. The reality is that sustainability will increasingly be part of every job, and it will be an intricate part of business itself. Nevertheless, we have managed to take it out and push it aside. The curriculum of the business school of the future will embed current sustainability topics throughout all classes and experiences, reaching all students rather than just a subsection. It will encourage students to question long-standing business assumptions and explore multiple possibilities and opportunities around these topics.

3. It will put impact front and centre

Business schools are quick to present lists of objectives and descriptions of what their teaching, research and projects will accomplish. But what actually happens thereafter? What impact do they actually have? The business school of the future will be more focused on impact rather than just outputs. What impact is that class having on students? What competencies are students truly developing? What impact is that research having in the short, medium and long term? What impact are faculty having on their students and in their fields? What impact are your graduates having on the world around them? How might this change the way we measure the success of business schools?

4. It will shift its culture

One of the challenges of a business degree isn't the content or structure but the underlying culture of the organizations that provide the degrees and the messages that are sent to their students throughout the course of study, both subtly and strongly. Of particular concern is the embedded acceptance that excess is good. This starts with the initial decision to do an MBA (high cost, return on investment, high-paying jobs, rankings based on salary) and continues throughout the curriculum (maximizing shareholder value, bigger is better, maximizing the bottom line). What kinds of businesses and graduates does this type of thinking aim to attract and create? What impact is it having on businesses and the potential for a more sustainable future? Forward-looking business schools will be much more purposeful about creating a culture that supports sustainability, and will shift from being focused purely on a single bottom line to acknowledging all three.

5. It will focus on transformative education

Rather than move into creating programmes that are shorter, business schools will focus on creating an environment that maximizes educational opportunities and the transformative development of its students. You might think that this is already the case, but it isn't always. Many students graduate without the skills and knowledge that they and their future places of work need moving forward. The way classes are taught, who is teaching the classes, the content and how those teachers are trained and are rewarded will all shift to ensure that students develop in a way that enables them to have a more meaningful role in the sustainability agenda.

6. It will become more multidisciplinary and connected

We live in a world, a business world, that is increasingly connected. One takes significant risks ignoring what is happening beyond one's own organization. Successful businesses of all types and sizes are increasingly not just identifying and considering the voices of their various stakeholders but actively engaging and working together with them to bring about positive change. Businesses are exploring solutions by bringing together exciting ideas from seemingly unrelated non-business disciplines, and partnering with different organizations to create true innovation. The business school of the future will increasingly represent and support the development of these types of abilities in its students to enable maximum impact on both an individual and collective level.

7. It will be more accessible and inclusive

By creating a more dynamic, relevant and multidisciplinary programme, the business school of the future will attract a much wider range of individuals, eliminating the need for diversity officers or quotas. It will be much more accessible to, and accepting of, individuals regardless of their background or business expertise, with a range of admission and pricing options. They will actively engage, learn from and contribute to their local communities. The objective is to create more inclusive business education, to attract the diversity of talent necessary to enable MBA programmes to really make a positive impact.

8. It will foster innovation

Generally speaking, business schools are not fostering innovation in business, especially when it comes to sustainability ... but they should be, and in the future they will be. Business schools are made up of a constantly changing group of interdisciplinary students, faculty experts and outside partners with a wide range of experience that could be put to use to explore opportunities and devise and implement solutions in the field of sustainability. The business school will become a test lab for new ideas. It will be at the forefront of environmental and social standards on campus, constantly pushing these forward. The business school would become not just a model but also an indispensable tool for the business sector and the wider community in making sustainability a reality.

9. It will influence change

The business school of the future will be part of a network of other business schools around the world, each made up of students, business partners, alumni, faculty, staff and their surrounding community. Together, they will become a power-ful force to bring about positive change at local, city, national, regional and international levels. Business schools will work more closely and efficiently with each other collaborating to create position statements and summaries of knowledge for use in dealing with pressing world issues. They will have the power to create movements, to bring people together quickly and efficiently to make things happen and will also prepare their students and graduates to be able to do the same in their daily lives, their careers and their communities. What if every busi-ness student wasn't just learning or talking about sustainability issues but actually exploring, testing and putting into practice innovative solutions to the world's business challenges? Imagine where we could be!

10. It will be anything we want it to be

Sustainability is an exciting field full of opportunity, in particu-lar for business schools, and should be embraced as such. Many of the business schools we know today will gradually become irrelevant and struggle to exist if they fail to adapt and change. Others will change so much that they will bear little resemblance to what they look like today. It is exciting to note that there are many different ways that schools can move forward, and rele-vant groups and networks of passionate and dedicated individu-als can help move schools forward – the future of management education is in our hands. Students themselves offer the most exciting opportunity to discuss and create that future, both on campus and beyond, and to prepare them not just to imagine what a more sustainable future will look like, but to be able to work with the organizations of today to get them to that place.

The future can be shaped into anything we want it to be; we just need to get on with it.

The ideas

The following 100 ideas are meant to provide inspiration to help shape the business degree of the future. While the original 100 ideas were posted as they were conceived, these have been organized to make it easier to follow. As previously mentioned, these ideas do not necessarily provide a specific roadmap forward, but rather inspiration about where we could go.

They start from the core, the student, training and developing that student into the best-prepared graduate possible. Second, the ideas look at the skills that the student will develop; third, the kind of curriculum they will be exposed to; and, fourth, the classroom environment within which they will be learning. How schools will actively engage in the sustainability agenda through their own programmes and operations is explored in Sections 5 and 6. Shaping a wider management education system that is more accessible and responsive is the focus of Section 7, and how schools engage in the local and international community are covered in Sections 8 and 9.

1   The student

Sustainability needs management education to become a space where true leaders are trained, leaders who have a better understanding of the world in which they do business, the people they do business with, their role within that environment, and can make better decisions because of it – for business, the planet and for society. What business school students look for and expect from business programmes will change dramatically. They will differ in the experiences they bring, connections they want to make, the careers they are building, and impacts they want to have in the world.

Idea 1. Suits

 Put a suit on someone and they look more respectable, smarter, more prepared. There is plenty of room in the world for a well-made, tailored suit. But a dark suit with a light-coloured shirt (the typical business-school uniform) also makes everyone in the room look similar. One could argue that the act of requiring students to wear suits to certain functions also encourages them to act, maybe even think, in a certain, similar way. It adds an element of formality that can stop students from speaking up, saying or asking what they want to say or ask, being open to discussion and exploration. It may even discourage those who don't own, have never worn, or are not interested in careers that require suits from applying in the first place.

If business schools are about bringing together a diverse group of people, sharing and connecting those differences to create a future workforce that can strengthen and innovate the business sector and make it more sustainable, then differences should be celebrated within the school. Creating a more casual dress environment (within reason) may provide a better setting for the sharing of information and insights, drawn both from successes and failures. It may give students the opportunity to focus on being what they are and not what the sector wants them to be.

This may seem like a small thing, but sometimes it is the small things that make the biggest difference.

Idea 2. Checking progress

 When it comes to educational and personal development, students will want to have a better understanding of where they stand when they start the programme and how they progress throughout it. Students will have access to a tool, updated in real time, which gives them insight as to where they are doing well and where they need to develop more. At the beginning of the programme the tool is populated with information related to the careers they are interested in, their strengths and weaknesses, the opinions of their past supervisors and colleagues. During the year, professors and fellow students will provide inputs. Students would use the tool to review their progress regularly, to help them choose which electives to take or activities to be engaged in to help strengthen some of the areas they are weak in or might need for their desired post-graduation job. Students will opt in to enable faculty to use their information to personalize their education. The tool would also connect students with other students, faculty and even alumni with similar strengths or weaknesses to collaborate with and learn from.

Such feedback could continue post-degree, providing continuous support for graduates at various stages of their careers. Schools could provide graduates with access to confidential assessments and provide data they can use themselves to develop and offer relevant educational programmes and assistance to their graduates.

Idea 3. Flexible course structure

A typical degree programme includes a range of three- to four-month courses organized in terms. Students meet for a few hours a week or a day to discuss that one topic. The future business degree could have a range of different, more flexible course formats. A few could be three months long, some could last the whole programme, and there could be a wide range of short courses that last just one week, or even 24 or 48 hours based on the topic and learning objectives. There could be traditional courses where you sit back, listen and participate, and others that are hands-on entrepreneurial sprints where you take an idea and put it into practice in one week or even 24 hours. A month could be dedicated just to looking at one topic in-depth across all courses. The curriculum will be flexible enough that new sections can be added based on demand throughout the year. This provides various ways to introduce materials and more importantly to engage students in business and sustainability discussions.

Idea 4. Reflection

Much of the time spent in business school is spent learning about and analysing the decisions that others have made, the numbers that others generated and the cases that others built. Although students are encouraged to bring their experiences into their studies, they aren't really given the time to reflect deeply on questions related to their own leadership style and the role they want to play, their values and what is important to them. But for education to be transformative and shape future sustainability leaders, reflection time is crucial.

Business schools will provide more structured space and time for students themselves to reflect and further develop their own self-awareness skills as future employees, managers and leaders by tapping into and using their own experiences as a key part of the learning process. Many assignments and opportunities will focus on giving students the chance to develop new habits and reflect at various levels on the work that they have done in the past and how the new knowledge they are learning in the class-room helps them to better understand decisions they made both before and during the degree. This will also help students to be able to reflect on their actions moving forward and continue to learn from their experiences throughout their careers.

Idea 5. Something different

 Taking time out of a career to study is a unique opportunity not just to learn, but also to explore topics you have always wanted to explore but have never had the time for. These help us see the world from different perspectives.

Future students could take part in a class called "Something Different". In this class, each student will choose something unrelated to the work that they are doing in the business degree to focus on. This could be a passion such as baking or surfing, learning about indigenous medicines or archaeology, exploring the world of salsa clubs or literature, or a side project such as a blog or creating a community garden. Once they choose their topic they will be asked to immerse themselves in that topic for the duration of the class based on the goal they have set them-selves: for example, to learn ballroom dancing by the end of the class or even write a novel. The students will then present what they have done and share some of the lessons learnt with fellow students. Many may find that their new business ideas, or even career directions, are inspired by their Something Different focus.

Idea 6. Life–work balance

 The environment in which we work in the future will be very different to what it is today. Fixed working days, long hours and short vacations will be replaced with more flexible options that see productivity and innovation increase substantially. There will be a renewed focus on what is important – a balance between work, life, family, friends, community—none of which come at the expense of any of the others. We will work smarter.

In order for this necessary change to happen, we will need our future leaders to have a better understanding and respect for the importance of life in the life–work balance and how they can help to create a business environment that accepts, supports and thrives on this shift in balance. Business schools will provide a range of experiences throughout the programme that will challenge students to think differently about balancing work and life at different stages of their career. They will expose students to a range of issues that those who work around them or eventually for them may experience throughout their working lives and how to deal with these. This includes, for example, the changes that having a family can have on your career, and how to provide a space to enable parents to be more successful at both roles.

Having a better understanding of these topics will enable students to create a work environment that brings out the best in those working within it.

Idea 7. Meditation

In an environment where individuals are constantly bombarded with information, how can future leaders be trained to focus and be more effective?

Meditation and business school are not two words that are usually heard together. However, a growing number of studies show that meditation can change the structure of the brain, leading to a boost in intelligence, that it helps people stay on tasks longer with fewer distractions, improves data retention, reduces stress, increases working memory and fosters creativity.

Future business programmes could integrate a range of meditation experiences and opportunities within the programme, to assist students in using this or other related techniques to focus and become more effective and mindful. They will, in turn, be more conscious of their impact on others as managers.

Idea 8. The portfolio

What is a CV? A CV is a short document that attempts to sum up your experience so far. But how effective is it at really communicating who you are, what you are capable of doing and what you bring to a job? Considering that most MBA applicants have CVs full of pretty lofty job titles; vice president of this, director of that, all by their mid-twenties, does communicating job titles really mean anything anymore? How do you best present your past, present and future abilities?

Career services within business degrees will also change in the future business school. One of the changes will be the way that students prepare their CVs. The CV itself will be redesigned, drawing inspiration from other fields, to become a stronger tool for communicating who you are, what you can bring to a job and what you want from a job. Formats will be drawn from a range of industries. Artists may inspire through their creation of visual portfolios of past projects, CVs could be arranged around specific skills (ones that the applicant has and wants) or based around proof of those competencies. They could involve videos or hands-on demonstrations. Whatever the format, they will aim to better represent the uniqueness and abilities of the individual.

Idea 9. Mentors

 Mentors are becoming an increasingly important tool for future leaders of all ages, both having a mentor of one's own and being one. Mentors can act as a sounding board for advice and recommendations, provide support and, when needed, a good kick to get going.

Business degrees will provide a more structured space focused on mentorship. Students will be paired with one or more mentors who will be with them not only throughout their programme but also as they move into their future career. These mentors could be leaders they look up to, others who have taken a similar path to them, or individuals who are working in a completely different field and who can provide some different perspectives. Students will also have the chance to be a mentor themselves during the programme, and beyond, to a current student or fellow alumnus. The programme will help students to better understand how to mentor and be mentored and how to benefit from these types of relationships throughout their careers.

Idea 10. To your health

Developing a good manager or leader is about many things, things that often have nothing to do with learning about finance, strategy or marketing. It is about shaping the whole person, how they see the world, how they collect information, communicate and make decisions. It is also about how they take care of themselves.

Placing a focus on health within a business degree may seem like a waste of precious time to some, but sending consistent messages to individuals that it's unhealthy to work 70-hour weeks, eat on the run, and not stay active is important not only for the individual, but for the business, and sustainability. In the long run, nobody benefits from this type of business culture, including business education.

One way of doing this could be through the addition of a new core course: a gym class. Every week students will come together to learn and play a different sport – soccer one week, yoga the next. This will serve multiple purposes, including exercise and stress release, of course, but also team building, socializing, networking and learning something new. You can also learn a lot about a person by how they approach the different challenges in gym class that may be outside their normal comfort zone.

Idea 11. The job search

For most, the post-graduation job search starts the day you arrive on campus. In fact, before students have even had a chance to sit back and think about their future, they have already missed recruiting for several industries. Students often don't have the chance to explore the full range of career options available to them and strict recruitment schedules often put additional pressures on students that take them away from the education itself.

Business schools will shift the focus away from the job search during the degree programme and instead allocate specific times throughout the programme, at the beginning, in the middle and at the end, that are dedicated solely to recruiting. During these selected times, rather than traditional classes, structured space will be given for students to think about their career goals in the short, medium and long term, to explore what success means to them, how to identify and take advantage of opportunities throughout their careers and make difficult choices. Students will have opportunities to interact with a wide range of potential employers, even shadow alumni and individuals working in careers that may be of interest. This is also an opportunity to be introduced to a range of career options students might not have initially thought of but to which they may be well suited.

The culture of the degree will no longer be one centred on finding a higher-paying job post-graduation, or choosing between consulting, finance or industry, but one that gives students the space and time to properly prepare and determine what their ideal career direction might be, and then make their move.

Idea 12. Leadership hub

 In business, a leader is often considered a senior executive or CEO of a large company. The suggested goal, therefore, if one wants to be seen as a leader in business, is to become like them, to reach those types of positions and to follow the actions and behaviours of these individuals.

But are these individuals all leaders? What makes a leader? Is it just their position? What about their actions, their skill-sets? What if we no longer need or can afford to have these types of leaders influencing the next generation of graduates, graduates we need to lead in different ways? What if you don't want to become that type of leader?

Students will be given more space to explore what leadership means to them, and what kind of leader they want to become. They will be exposed to a wide range of types of leaders, to explore a variety of styles and to help them to develop into the type of leader they want to be. Business schools will have a permanent space that will regularly host individuals and groups that are considered leaders in their fields including non-business fields. This could be sports, arts, music, sciences, or any field. An Olympian, a Nobel Prize winner, a community activist, or a leading pastry chef all have a number of traits that have enabled them to succeed individually, and as part of a team, which could influence and be part of the skill-set of a new generation of sustainable business leaders.

2 The skills

The business school of the future will shift to put a much stronger emphasis on the so-called 'soft' skills to prepare its graduates to be better day-to-day managers, team members, more effective communicators and listeners, and able to better engage and inspire those around them. Graduates will know how to collaborate, make connections and to bring about change. They will learn how to balance life and work, their time, their energy, to be able to learn from their mistakes, and continue to develop throughout their careers.

Idea 13. Risk taking and failure

The lessons during a typical business degree revolve around best practice and success stories. But what about the "failures"? For most of us, there isn't a lot of space for risk taking and failure in our professional lives. Risk is seen as something bad, something to be identified and mitigated against, something to avoid.

But great things often come from taking risks: new ideas, new opportunities and new insights. Many professionals will tell you they failed many more times than they succeeded and often feel they would have never succeeded if they hadn't taken certain risks, failed a few times first and then learnt from those "failures". Both individuals and a business can benefit from not only creating an environment where they and others can make mistakes and learn from them, but also one that encourages and develops these processes. Businesses increasingly need graduates who aren't afraid of questioning assumptions or testing new ideas, graduates that can help create a culture and environment in business that supports risk taking in a constructive way.

Business schools will have a course about smart risk taking in both the student's personal and professional lives. It will look at what risk is and why it is good/bad, and how we can benefit from smart risk taking. It will explore examples of "failures" in companies of all shapes and sizes, how they came about, and how they were handled, including how failure is viewed and defined within different company cultures. The course will also explore the way other organizations, businesses and individuals create an environment that encourages smart risk taking and learns from its mistakes.

Students will have opportunities to explore their own experiences with failure as well as access to a range of practical activities that would enable them to explore taking risks in a relatively safe classroom environment, in their personal lives and on special projects.

Idea 14. Skill sharing

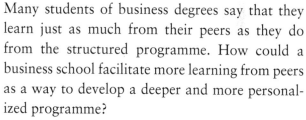

Many students of business degrees say that they learn just as much from their peers as they do from the structured programme. How could a business school facilitate more learning from peers as a way to develop a deeper and more personalized programme?

Students, staff, faculty and alumni will have the opportunity to make a note in their profiles of a limited number of special skills or particular interests or knowledge that they would be willing to share. This could be basic skills that are useful during the programme such as how to create complex spreadsheets, public speaking, budgeting, creating a website or time management. It could be more specialized expertise such as how to scale up business ideas, legal and tax advice or hiring employees. The skills could be around different career options such as careers in consulting, finance or NGOs, or non-business skills such as how to grow a vegetable garden, learning to play a musical instrument, preparing for a baby or brewing your own beer.

A system will be put in place to encourage and enable members of the university community to connect with others with the knowledge they are interested in. This could be further developed into a special "time-bank", where students, staff, graduates and even business partners and the community will be invited to join. As part of the time-bank, individuals will provide a range of professional services for free based on their expertise and skill-sets. In exchange, when they need help with something they can tap into the system to use the time they have accumulated, helping others to get help themselves.

Idea 15. Soft skills become hard skills

The business degree is very much based around the so-called "hard skill" courses. Courses in accounting, finance, strategy and marketing dominate the majority of course hours with the "soft skills" courses of leadership and change management often allocated to just a few electives. Although the hard skills are important, it is the soft skills that will help graduates to succeed in their careers moving forward, and which will be increasingly important in the business environment of the future.

Business schools could flip the curriculum, putting the soft skill courses at the core. All graduates would still graduate with the basic "hard" knowledge that they need in the business community, but the emphasis would be on creating better managers and leaders with interdisciplinary knowledge, the ability to work with others across borders and to understand and put sustainability approaches into practice.

Idea 16. From negotiation to consensus building

 The class in negotiation is one of the most popular electives for business students around the world. The class is focused on maximizing your share of the pie, often at the expense of the other party. Many see it as a course on how to win.

However in today's business environment, graduates need to understand a wide range of methods at their disposal, often more effective methods, for resolving disputes and moving business relationships forward between different groups, whether that be another business partner or a local community. This includes, but is not limited to, consensus building, alternative dispute resolution, facilitation and mediation. This new course would cover negotiation as part of a range of different approaches and techniques that a manager can use, explore how to identify when to use them and how to use them effectively.

Idea 17. Communication 101

 Not enough emphasis is placed on communication skills, a key skill-set which differentiates effective managers from average ones. Communication skills are crucial in being able to lead, sell ideas, gather support and make things happen. Despite this, business schools are currently in the process of taking out many of the opportunities that currently exist for students to further develop and explore these skills.

Rather than assume these are lessons that students are learning during their time in the programme, this course deals with the topic explicitly. This course, which will last the duration of the degree, will focus on a range of communication skills that are necessary in a day-to-day work environment in order to create future leaders who are able to more effectively manage their time, engage those around them and make an impact.

Students will explore how to communicate an idea or message through various presentation techniques, including how to present an idea simply and effectively to a wide range of different audiences. The course will look at how to organize and facilitate effective meetings, how to contribute in meaningful ways, how to assess the strengths and weaknesses of those working around you and how to give and receive constructive feedback and criticism. The course will help students to develop active listening skills, the ability to take in information, to understand multiple positions and to frame problems in order to begin to explore solutions. A large part of the class will focus on cross-cultural communication.

Idea 18. Thinking small

 The next big idea; the next big company; bigger is better – these are underlying messages that thread through many business programmes. But not everything needs to be big to be successful, impactful and desirable. In fact, much of the world of business is small. Small and medium enterprises make up the majority of employers, big companies are made up of many small ones acquired over time and much of the technology, innovations and new ideas are coming from small companies. Graduates who are interested in entrepreneurship will often need to start small even though they may aspire to something bigger.

In the future, the business degree will give equal importance to small business in all its forms, including cooperatives, family businesses and SMEs. There will be an emphasis on how to run and manage small businesses and provide space for entrepreneurs with small businesses that have no need or desire to grow on how to keep their businesses small but strong.

Thousands of small ideas and small businesses can be more impactful in moving sustainability forward and engaging communities through the development of innovative ideas and making a difference on the ground than one or two large ones. Shouldn't they be given the same level of respect?

Idea 19. From competition to collaboration

 Today's business and world challenges are too complex for one organization to tackle alone. Furthermore, many businesses face the exact same or very similar challenges. Because of this, businesses that used to be competitors are now also partners, collaborating on projects that enable both parties to move forward with their respective sustainability strategies.

This new course will focus on the shift from competition to collaboration. It will explore questions such as how to work with other businesses on a range of different initiatives. These could be research projects, or initiatives that involve working with competitors, working with businesses from a range of different industries, or working on voluntary programmes. It will also provide students with the tools to determine what kind of collaboration might work best in different situations as well as the rules of engagement and making sure all parties contribute and gain from the collaboration.

Universities themselves need to strengthen their ability to effectively collaborate with different organisations such as business, NGOs and governments. Activities in this class will also provide opportunities for students and faculty to help develop new and strengthen any existing collaborations in which the school is engaged.

Idea 20. Questioning assumptions

 The business world is full of assumptions about the way that we currently do things, that the way we have always done something is the best way to do it. But what if it isn't, and what if a new way would not only be better for business but for the planet and society as well?

Business schools will have a class called "Questioning Assumptions". This could be a separate class and/or be a small part of every class students take throughout their degree programme. This class would identify and explore a series of widely held assumptions in the world of business. This could include small ones we make on a day-to-day basis, large-industry-held assumptions that guide product development or the way businesses are run, or fundamental ones such as what is the role of the corporation. During this class, students will explore these assumptions in order to better understand where they come from and then proceed to take them apart and provide alternative viewpoints that could be used to build up new and more effective models.

Idea 21. Smarter teams

 Many business school programmes require students to work in teams, since teams are an important part of the "real world". However, a lot of basic teamwork skills are learnt on the fly, without any formal guidance. What makes an effective team and what kinds of team do we need in order to be more effective at bringing sustainability into all our discussions?

Business schools should not only become spaces that create individual change-makers, but also prepare its graduates to be able to work together better, smarter, to bring about even more positive change. Teams in the future business school will be more diverse. They will be encouraged and enabled to create everyday experiences, processes and objectives that empower better decisions by individuals within the group and by the group itself. These decisions will take into account multiple perspectives and consider the implications of those decisions. This could include rewards, structures and deliverables. Students will then take these experiences to help them rethink the way teams work when they start at their new workplaces.

Idea 22. Plus one

 We often hear that we need graduates who can think outside the box, who can take a 360° view of a challenge and offer and analyse a range of possible solutions. However, many of the assignments reward the first and most obvious answers without pushing students to explore the topic further. Many lessons relating to social and environmental issues are never raised because they don't make it into that first answer.

Business classes will be taught in different ways that encourage students to think about the challenges and the solutions more broadly. One tool for facilitating this type of learning would be a tool called "Plus One". For every answer or solution offered in an assignment, project or class discussion, students will need to offer a second alternative. This will be done even when the question has a "clear" right or wrong answer in order to encourage students to question long-standing assumptions. This will push students to dive deeper into the topics, to not necessarily settle on the first or most obvious answer and to explore more than one possible scenario.

Idea 23. Influence

 Influence is a powerful tool. We as individuals are influenced by the never-ending stream of messages we hear and see in the world around us. These messages, how we interpret them and the importance we assign to them, shape and guide our actions in our jobs, as consumers, and in our everyday life. At the same time, we have the power to influence others with what we say and how we act, both for good and for bad. With an increase in social media and the almost instant sharing of information, it is important that future leaders understand what is influencing their behaviours (and that of others) at a conscious and subconscious level and how to manage this.

Business schools will have a module focused on the topic of influence as well as the wider culture that that influence can shape. This module will look at both how we can better understand, filter and deal with the influences around us. It will also look at the positive power of influence to change the minds and behaviours of others within a business and in society as a whole.

3 The curriculum

The days of sitting in a classroom, listening to a person at the front of the room for hours on end, are over. Instead, education will be about learning how to tap into information, to make connections, and to engage. Business degrees will focus on providing a range of contexts within which to learn and apply these lessons, ensuring that graduates don't just graduate with the theoretical knowledge they need, but the ability to apply it across a range of situations.

Idea 24. Here and now

A large percentage of the teaching hours of a business degree are focused on teaching students based on what happened in the past.

By the time a lesson makes it into a textbook or is written up into a case study, years may have passed. While there are many lessons to be learnt from the past, students and graduates need to be able to deal with what is happening now. Business schools are educating managers for a future business reality that we know little or nothing about, but one that students will need to be able to respond to – and ideally shape.

Business schools will have a class called "Today". This short class takes place every morning before core courses start. The class looks at current events as they happen and explores what they mean for business, how business should/could respond, exploring potential opportunities and/or risks both now and in the future.

For example, an NGO releases a report that negatively affects company X. In Today's class, students will look at this report and explore how they think company X should respond to the news and track what the company actually does over the upcoming days. In the upcoming weeks, a representative of company X could be invited into the class to discuss their approach.

The class would be interdisciplinary, mixing students from different degree programmes, and faculty would be encouraged to attend as well. The room would be set up with students sitting in small groups around tables, each discussing the same or different topics.

Idea 25. Flavour of the month

Every year, despite what is happening in the world around us, business school education stays largely the same. Similar classes are taught in a similar way. How do we create a business school that responds and adapts to, and actively participates in, the world around it while preparing students and professionals to work in that world?

Each year, individual or groups of business schools will focus on a specific theme. This special programme will happen in parallel with the traditional programmes offered but will be open to a wider audience and involve a number of outside partners. Each school can choose its theme based on issues that are of particular importance to its community, country, region or global issues at that time. This could include conflicts, political issues, environmental or social issues, and even new discoveries. This shorter programme (one week to one year) will include a range of events, courses, conversations and projects specifically aimed at raising students' awareness of that particular issue as it is relevant today, and discussing how to move that issue forward.

For students, these programmes will not only create graduates who are knowledgeable and ready to work to solve these challenges today, but to apply these skills to other issues as they encounter them in their work. These short programmes will also gather momentum and act as a central, neutral space to shape discussions around the topic in question and move the issue forward with the business community. Students and professionals as well as alumni would be invited to participate.

Idea 26. Plug and play

How, in the classroom, can you bring topics to life that are dynamic, multifaceted and constantly changing? In the future, a variety of organizations in particular fields will create regularly updated mini-lectures on the subject on which they specialize, which can be used within business school programmes globally. For example, a lecture on managing conservation projects in rural communities could connect with an organization working on the ground and this could be delivered live to various schools or as a recording to be used in class. As another example, a course exploring reporting standards could connect with the Global Reporting Initiative to deliver this lecture using up-to-date information and examples.

These mini-lectures could be used to build up a core curriculum, supplement a student's learning, provide different perspectives on an issue being dealt with in the curriculum, and make up a new breed of live, video case studies which could become a staple in business school teaching.

Idea 27. Start something

Some of the most popular courses during the MBA are those related to entrepreneurship. A large number of students and graduates dream of one day starting their own business. The business school of the future will provide an opportunity for students to not just learn about starting a business but to actually start one during their time on campus.

There will be a series of 24/48-hour entrepreneurship boot camps throughout the programme. At each boot camp a group of students will present their business or project idea and the rest of the students will help, in the period of 24–48 hours, to get that business idea off the ground (basic business plan, website, prototypes, etc.). In addition to business students and faculty, students from other disciplines such as engineering, design and advisors, funders, etc. will be present to assist and contribute. The students could then put into practice their small business idea or project for the duration of the programme (and beyond, if desired).

Idea 28. Travelling without travelling

 Ideally, in order to become a more globally aware leader, you would spend your degree travelling around the world, exposing yourself to different business cultures. However, this isn't always feasible due to financial and time constraints.

Instead, in order to ensure that students have a better understanding of different cultures and the realities, opportunities and challenges that exist when doing business around the world, students will have access to a special Global Centre. Staff from the Global Centre will regularly come into the classroom, or invite others into the classroom, to provide a cultural context to the different cases and topics that are being explored. The Centre will provide a space for students to meet to learn about different cultures for assignments, for general interest and before going on exchanges, internships, interviews, or into full-time work. This office will have connections with embassies, cultural centres, alumni and current students as well as schools in other countries that can provide additional resources and support.

It will also have access to virtual-reality platforms that can provide an additional opportunity for cultural immersion.

Idea 29. Connecting faculty

The way that faculty introduce the topic of sustainability in their courses, and the way that they approach the topic (or fail to) sends very strong and clear messages to students about its importance. As such, it represents one of the major challenges in ensuring students are not only fluent in the language of sustainability, but know how to put it into practice. However, many faculty members feel that they do not have the knowledge, the time or the space to further explore this topic or feel that it has little relevance to the work that they are doing. Alternatively, they think it is already covered elsewhere in the curriculum.

In the future, faculty will be connected virtually in ways that will enable them to collaborate and learn from each other around innovations in sustainability. Through this platform, faculty from across universities around the world, or within a specific school, will be able to connect with others teaching the same course to share course material, experiences and resources. They can join together to start new collaborations, especially across disciplines, to create stronger, more effective courses. Virtual brown-bag lunches will give faculty the chance to learn more about different approaches to embedding sustainability into their courses.

Idea 30. Labs

Business schools have a range of research centres doing cutting-edge research. There are Centres for Women in Business, Centres for Ethics and Society, Centres for Entrepreneurship, to name but a few. And, although many of these centres do some innovative work, many have a very limited impact on their students, on their communities or even on their fields. So how can we rethink the business school "centre" to make it more impactful for all involved?

Centres will be reinvented to become "labs": a Women in Business Lab, an Ethics Lab. Rather than bring together groups of individual researchers publishing papers, labs will be much more action-oriented and involve a wider range of individuals. Special projects will bring together multiple faculty and researchers to collaboratively explore a problem, offer solutions, test them, and put them in place when possible.

Labs will actively engage the student body. Each lab will conduct one or a range of courses relating to its specific field of study. Students will not only be accepted into their business programme but could also have the opportunity to apply to one or more specific labs on campus depending on their interests. During their programme, they will then get special access to the work happening in that lab and contribute to it. They could also become a connection between the lab and the student body to share lessons and opportunities and current research.

Idea 31. Modularizing core courses

In choosing specializations and electives, students have more opportunities than ever to tailor their MBA ... but within limits. The core courses they take generally allow for very little personalization, and every student enrolled in, let's say a finance course, needs to take the exact same course regardless of their past experiences in the subject, their current interests, or future use.

Most MBA programme officers already note that the curriculum is full and that it is very difficult to add anything new into the programme. In the future, in addition to questioning the relevance of the material already being taught, business degrees may also look at changing the way courses are taught.

One solution to this is to change the structure of the core courses. Rather than one long course that everyone sits through, a core course would be divided into three parts. Take the finance class, for example. The first part of the course brings all the students together for an introduction and overview of the topic. For the second part, the group is divided into two: the first group would explore advanced topics for those interested in careers in finance or those with experience in this area who want to go more in depth; the second group would be those students who will explore the subject from a more practical perspective. Students would be free to attend one or both streams. At the end of this second part of the class, all students would come back together to finish off the course.

Idea 32. Impactful courses

There are so many strong courses offered by business school programmes around the world, courses that push students to think and act in different ways and are effective at creating more knowledgeable and capable students. Many passionate faculty have developed innovative courses exploring a range of sustainability topics. The catch is that they aren't necessarily all offered by the programme that you have decided to attend.

Business schools will enable students to take any course from any school around the world. A system will be developed to identify which courses are particularly impactful and relevant. Students would then have the opportunity to either attend the class in person or online. Some would be open to all, others may have limited spaces allocated based on application, for example. Faculty of these courses may have the opportunity to go on a "course tour", where they give their class to students in different schools throughout the school year or partner with other faculty to deliver it. In this way, students have access to the best classes on offer on a particular topic.

Idea 33. Shifts

Education is, for the most part, predictable. At any given moment you know what classes you have, the assignments you have to get done or are coming up, when your next exam or presentation is. But the world students enter into after graduation is anything but predictable and one of the skills that employers look for, and which businesses exploring sustainability need, is adaptability. So how could we further develop this in business students?

The business school of the future, in addition to its standard curriculum, will have a special series of modules called "Shifts". Basically, at different points in the curriculum students will be put into an unexpected situation that they need to resolve. They will have no idea when these will happen, or what the situation will be. Some could involve groups of students while others could be specifically tailored to a student based on skills the student is looking to develop. There could be countless different ways of presenting a "Shift" for a student. A Shift could consist of a student to prepare a presentation for the Dean in 24 hours, or taking over the management of a special project for a short period of time, or finding a solution to an emergency – or even being sent to a foreign country on a special mission. They will all be of short duration and students, depending on the project, will be judged on how they approached the situation and what they took out of the experience in addition to how successful they were.

Idea 34. Long-term thinking

 Increasingly, much of business and business teaching is focused on short-term measures of value often at the expense of the long-term thinking that can create stronger and more sustainable organizations. How can we ensure that business school graduates put proper emphasis on long-term thinking and planning, and understand how to balance this with the medium and short term?

The future business degree will look specifically at long-term thinking. This course will explore how to think and plan long-term in a business environment that is increasingly focused on the short term. It will explore what long-term thinking and goals look like, including visionary goals and how to plan these and eventually reach them. Also to be explored are the complexities of business decisions made today and the impacts that they will have in the longer term. Students will be encouraged to discuss and create new business models and products that focus and succeed based on longer-term thinking. The course will also look at how to balance short-term expectations with long-term goals, and the different incentive structures present in terms of behaviours and organizational cultures that promote short-term thinking and what could be done to change these.

Idea 35. The slow MBA

Everything is getting faster. Cars go faster, time seems to go faster, businesses rise up and fall down faster. The MBA is a roller-coaster ride. Students are thrown more work than they can possibly finish effectively, and more opportunities to learn than they could ever really take advantage of. This is what the business environment is like. But should it be and will it be in the future? Studies show that the "more and faster is better" approach to work is not true, and that in fact more hours of work does not make us more productive. Rather than "lighting fires" under employees, increasingly the role of managers could be to create more space to explore, especially when innovation matters, as it does in sustainability.

The Slow Food movement was founded to counter the rise of fast food and fast life, the disappearance of local food traditions and people's dwindling interest in the food they eat, where it comes from, how it tastes and how our food choices affect the rest of the world. Perhaps what we need is a Slow MBA movement, founded to celebrate the field of management and engage schools to provide time for students to linger on topics and lessons that interest them, space to think about the implications of their actions, and guidance to plan and ponder the impact that they want to have on the world around them. Maybe we all just need to slow down.

4 The classroom

The future business degree isn't just about what is being taught, but how that information is being taught. It is about the context and environment for learning and development. In the future, efforts will be made to ensure that all students get the most out of the experience, that spaces, schedules, techniques and methods are all adapted to ensure maximum impact for each student.

Idea 36. In the mood for learning

Today, most students already carry some sort of smart device around with them on campus. In the future, these devices will collect information about the mood of the students, whether they are stressed or relaxed, overwhelmed or engaged. Other students and teachers will have access to this information and will be able to gauge the state of their team members or the student body as a whole and adapt messages, support and experiences accordingly. Educational content itself, as well as the teaching methods and materials, could be automatically adapted, based on the moods or different states of mind of the students.

Idea 37. Creative space

When it comes to solving the world's, and business's, challenges, creativity, generating new ideas and "thinking outside the box" are all skills that future graduates need. Despite the fact that most business school students do not come from a traditional "creative" background, it is important that they explore how to be inspired by the world around them and, more importantly, to better understand how they can tap into creativity tools, their own and others', to come up with new ideas, products, processes and projects in their respective jobs. Creativity is a skill we all have and use to varying degrees, but perhaps the business school is more effective at marginalizing this skill than developing it in ways that are beneficial to one's chosen career.

Business schools will have a creative space on campus to encourage the development and use of these skills in their students. This highly interactive space will contain a constantly changing supply of "inspiration" from around the business and non-business world. Students will have the chance to enter the space to explore their own creativity and different methods of tapping into it, to see what inspires them and how, and to help them to put that inspiration to good use in their work now and in the future. The space will also explore creativity tools, brainstorming, problem solving and idea generation. Established and emerging professionals from different fields will be invited to share their work. It will be updated through partnerships with relevant local organizations, including museums, galleries and theatres, which will both send individuals to work on campus with the students and invite the students to their spaces to explore their work.

Idea 38. Rethinking the classroom

 The typical business school classroom is an amphitheatre. Students sit in rows all facing forward, focused on the important person at the front in the middle.

Learning, however, is an interactive process. Many business schools proudly advertise the diversity of their student body as an opportunity to network but, more importantly, learn from each other. The goal of the classroom set-up, therefore, should be to facilitate this kind of learning, meeting and collaboration. It should also be to encourage different kinds of learning for different kinds of students and subject matters.

Business school classrooms will not be amphitheatres but more collaborative spaces that encourage discussion and learning. They will be made up of, for example, a series of small tables and chairs, easily movable around the space. The "seating" chart will change constantly to encourage students to meet and learn from different sets of peers. The walls will be lined with giant whiteboards to provide the option for groups to brainstorm and explore topics more visually. The space will be flexible and adaptable, depending on the needs of a particular class or group of students.

Idea 39. Reinventing the textbook

 We live in a world where information is available when we want it, where we want it and in whatever shape or form we want it. Business schools train students to become the leaders of today and tomorrow . . . but do this using the textbooks of yesterday. At the same time, the internet is so full of information there is an increasing need to filter it in a way that is usable for the classroom.

The textbook of the future will provide base information about a particular topic and then give links to expand that learning. These links would include different current perspectives on a particular issue, allowing students to develop a well-rounded view of the topic. It would also include a range of examples of current applications, updated regularly, to see how this information is used in practice. Once students get through the "required" portion of the reading, there would be several opportunities to continue by following a series of pre-filtered links that may take them in a different direction of their choosing, so that they do not just learn the lesson but become immersed and find an aspect of that learning that means something to them. A student that chooses to continue further may be linked to possible internships, project opportunities, conferences or even alumni working in that specific topic. Students themselves can rate links, suggest new links and comment throughout. In this way, the textbook becomes a living document, something more interactive and real, more useful and more personal, which allows students to organize and use information differently.

Idea 40. Turning off

 It is amazing how many things you can do at once in a classroom. You can follow a lecture, write notes, check the internet for information relating to the class . . . or relating to where you are going to go out for dinner tonight. You can chat with your friends in the classroom or on the other side of the planet, start doing homework for another class, play games . . . you can do a lot of things that have nothing to do with the class at all. As we are increasingly addicted to being connected 24/7, future students will need to learn how to just turn off and listen.

Students will be asked to leave their cell phones, computers and all other devices at the door for courses where they are not necessary. Without the distraction of computers, and everyone else being on their computers, student will (hopefully) become more present, contribute more, and reflect more.

The computer and more specifically the internet is an incredible tool, but also an incredibly distracting one. We need a generation of leaders who are better listeners and observers, who are focused and participate fully; and their educational experience will be richer because of it.

Idea 41. Subscription service

Walk through the halls of most MBA pro-grammes and you will see piles of today's edition of the *Financial Times* or this week's *The Economist* waiting to be picked up by students. The training of more interdisciplinary, well-rounded and knowledgeable managers will also include exposing them to a wider range of perspectives and news stories that connect with the business world they are committed to working in.

Universities will offer their students, faculty, staff and alumni a special service to encourage them to read and think about the topics that interest them in different ways. Based on preferences set into the system, this special subscription service will regularly send them to a range of publications that provide unique and innovative points of view on topics that are of interest to them. This could be articles, blogs, magazines or books from around the world.

Often the inspiration for a new idea, a new product, even a new career direction, comes from something unexpected that you have read.

Idea 42. Flexible spaces

Imagine a learning environment made up of a range of flexible spaces. Walls can be put up and taken down in minutes, tables and chairs rearranged in a variety of different ways or taken away altogether to create a large open space. Parking lots can be turned into reception spaces or athletic grounds in the evening. A lounge for socializing can be turned into a classroom once the break is over. Walls can be transformed from decorative spaces to collaborative brainstorming whiteboards with a flip of a switch. Furniture can be rearranged to change a group setting to a quiet corner for an individual to study or work, have a one-on-one meeting or make a private call. Traditionally unused or under-used spaces, such as a roof, will be transformed into multi-use spaces, such as a community rooftop garden with seating for eating, studying or even small classes.

The university with windowless classrooms will exist no longer. Spaces will incorporate natural light and sustainable-building concepts, and thus increase morale and productivity. Even office spaces will adapt, allowing individual employees' desks to be moved around so that they can work together; they can even be set up outside work on a sunny day.

Idea 43. The ultimate library

 A library is a place for discovery. But libraries in schools are often filled with dusty books and journals and are more popular as a space to study than a place to learn and discover. How can we turn business school libraries into dynamic learning environments for students?

The library will be a more central part of the business degree for students. Courses will take place in the library teaching students how to find, filter and question information in an environment that is increasingly overflowing with it. Collections will be brought to life, curated by students themselves, faculty, guest business leaders and the community to feature certain topics, themes or educate about current events. The library will include event spaces, writing areas and conversation areas, and will become a central space for students on all programmes.

Books will be taken off the shelves, spread on tables with covers exposed to encourage students to take one, sit down and flick through it. Platforms will help students explore online information in more focused ways. The librarians will become the best-known individuals on the campus, not only knowledgeable about how to help you find information you are looking for, but gifted at introducing students to information they never knew they needed.

The world is feeling the loss of bricks-and-mortar bookstores. Perhaps by exploring how to create an engaging space of discovery in business schools, these schools can play a role in bringing back the love of libraries and bookstores, and shift the perceptions of the thousands of business managers and leaders that graduate every year.

Idea 44. Virtual and instant

 A business school will have a technology centre, working in collaboration with many of the leading-edge technological firms. It will be open to students from a range of other, non-business disciplines to facilitate collaboration on projects.

This space will go beyond providing computers with the latest software and training. Students will be able to tap into a network of alumni, business partners and other students around the world to instantly give or provide feedback, collaborate, learn and share. Intelligent computer programmes, or virtual connections with other students and faculty around the world, will give students one-on-one tutoring and testing on anything from financial concepts to interview preparation and learning a new language, 24 hours a day. The possibilities will be endless.

Idea 45. Upside down

Not a day goes by without some mention of Massive Open Online Courses (MOOCs) and how they are taking over business education. These open courses, which are given to unlimited numbers of students simultaneously online, are often mentioned in discussions about what the future business degree will look like.

Business schools will see students learning business basics via online lectures and courses outside of the classroom through MOOCs and other online platforms. This would then free up the day to attend a range of courses that focus on bringing this information to life, clarifying what the concepts mean, discussing them and questioning them, exploring how to apply them and working on projects that give students the chance to put these lessons into practice.

The future leaders that we need will not be created by simply sitting in front of a computer. While MOOCs have their place, we need individuals who have a range of skills and experiences that no online course can provide. This dual approach will allow faculty to tap into similar new and innovative tools to strengthen rather than replace their courses.

Idea 46. Centres for rapid prototyping

Business schools will have Centres for Rapid Prototyping, or CRPs. In these spaces, students will be able to take a business idea, and create a quick prototype which can be further explored, shared, tested and used and which will allow students to quickly iterate through multiple versions of that idea. A close partnership with other disciplines within the university will give business students access to engineering, art, architecture and other students (and vice versa) who would be available to help develop prototypes. 3D printers and a range of state-of-the-art technology and innovative sustainable materials will be on hand for use. The centre will produce no waste as the materials used will be reused, recycled or sold.

Students will have access to real and virtual worlds which they can create or join to test out new business models, products, campaigns or solutions in real time and based on up-to-date global statistical information. Students will also have the opportunity to scale up production and even sell prototypes on campus and beyond.

The local business community would also have access to this space and the students to test out their own ideas for new products and get feedback. The centres will provide a range of short courses and opportunities for students of all experience levels to learn about testing out ideas with opportunities to work on a range of products with other students and external organizations.

5 The programme

The business school of the future will be much more flexible than it is today. It will provide more flexibility in terms of the kinds of programmes on offer, whether they be short, long, aimed at students from a particular discipline, focused on a particular part of their career, or available over a lifetime. They will provide flexibility in terms of how they are delivered, where they are being taught, when they are being taught and by whom. They will respond more quickly to the needs of the wider business community and change in response to these requirements.

Idea 47. Create your own adventure

When something is made specifically for you, based on your needs and wants, it can be customized to fit perfectly. What if a business degree were the same? What if, when you entered a degree, you could be sure that it would provide you with what you wanted and needed, and be flexible and adaptable enough to change based on the new directions you might take, new skills you want to develop or weakness you want to address? What if your business degree were tailor-made for you?

In the future, students will be able to build their own programmes from scratch and present their plans to their chosen business school or schools for approval. They will have flexibility on the location, which courses they take, which assignments they complete and how they complete them. They can build new courses from scratch, focus on a particular topic of interest and adapt parts of their programme as they go. They can also propose how long they have to complete the degree and whether they will do it part- or full-time. At the end of their programme, they will bring together the work they have done in front of a panel of peers, faculty, perhaps business partners, and demonstrate their progress over the course of the degree to determine whether or not they graduate.

Business schools will shift from being seen as providers to partners in education. Faculty and staff will be seen as learning counsellors, helping students to develop their career goals, understand their strengths and weaknesses, and customize their programme accordingly.

Idea 48. The interdisciplinary MBA

 Sustainability is an interdisciplinary topic, and, as such, managers need to have a wider understanding of the systems that affect business and that business itself affects, whether that be economic, social or environmental. Business schools will offer fully interdisciplinary programmes that not only expose students to a range of different business and non-business topics, but teach them how to move between them and to connect them together.

Students would take the majority of their classes from across a whole university, from social sciences to engineering, anthropology and design or natural sciences, to provide a range of different perspectives. New business courses would be developed that combine similar courses in other disciplines, bringing together faculty and different sets of students to explore a topic from many different angles.

In this programme, for example, a student interested in working in business in the medical profession could take classes offered in the medical school and have the opportunity to shadow medical students in a hospital to get a better understanding of the industry and those working in that industry. Students would also be tasked with assignments that would help to connect the different disciplines, explore opportunities to collaborate across them and explore interdisciplinary sustainability solutions.

Idea 49. Memberships

 Do the business schools of the future need to be defined by degree-based educational programs? Could they instead become a service that provides individuals and businesses with an ongoing number of on-demand products, such as training and advisory services, which are up to date and relevant?

Business schools will become membership-based programmes. The business schools themselves might have a range of different types of memberships and membership levels for individuals of all ages and for businesses. Memberships would last months, years, even a lifetime, and give members access to a range of services whenever the individual wants or is ready for that service.

Businesses who are members can co-create courses with the university they are a member of to co-deliver to employees from that company, or open up to employees from other companies. Individuals and businesses can choose to be a member of one or several different business schools based on reputation, specific expertise areas or location. Sharing membership benefits could lead to a new model for international business school partnerships.

Idea 50. Peer-to-peer MBA

 Courses are created and delivered by faculty. But what if this were flipped? What if it were the students themselves who created spaces, both physical and virtual, where they explored topics of importance to them within the degree? These spaces would engage students 24 hours

a day and seven days a week, enabling them to connect, contribute and learn whenever and for as much time and in whatever way they desire. Students would become both creators and consumers of lessons. Students with an expertise in a particular area would become facilitators of learning for fellow students. Students would organize collective meet-ups, field trips, events and guest speakers to bring discussions to life, as they happen through the platform created by the school. Faculty would still play a key role, engaging with students actively through this platform, providing additional guidance and direction, kickstarting new discussions and steering students.

Idea 51. Crowdsourcing

Businesses are constantly changing and adapting, or even being created, in response to new opportunities, new risks and new technologies. Currently, business schools make changes to their curriculum every two to five years. How can business schools also take advantage and respond quickly to new opportunities as they arise with a range of innovative and flexible programmes that serve the needs of the business community?

In the future, business school programme content and topics, in particular in executive programmes, would be crowdsourced by executives, alumni, potential and current students and business partners, and developed in real time in order to ensure that they cover the training needs of the business community as they arise. They would explore, via an online platform and in person, what should be taught, for how long, and in what way. Enrolled students would continue to give real-time feedback, which could result in changes to the rest of the curriculum, and strengthen the course for students enrolling in the same programme for the next year.

Idea 52. Minors

The good, and bad, thing about a business degree, in particular the MBA, is that it immerses you in a world of business for months. Most business students have very little exposure to anything non-business-focused throughout their degree programme. If we need a new generation of leaders who have a multidisciplinary skill-set, shouldn't we expose business students to other disciplines throughout their programme?

In the future, students will be required to complete a minor in a topic outside of the business school. If the business school is part of a larger university, they will have access to programmes on campus. For other schools, students would have the opportunity to take courses at schools in their city, in their country or internationally, based on their interests. For example, a student interested in the fashion industry could do a minor at a fashion school in London, New York or Milan. Other students may choose minors in anthropology or engineering.

Idea 53. The curated MBA

Students in the future will have the opportunity to personalize their degree programme. Many of the previous ideas have discussed this point. But how can a student know what is the best way to personalize their degree in order to best prepare them for the career they aspire to?

Individuals or groups of alumni and professionals will be able to put together packages showing how they would recommend completing an MBA based on different, very specific, career choices. This could include the courses they took, events they participated in and the skills to focus on developing. These curated packages would include general tips for the students about which experiences were most useful and those that were less so. Students can tap into this network for inspiration in order to create their own personalized degree.

Idea 54. The retired MBA

Many individuals retire at 60+. These individuals are extremely knowledgeable, have an incredible skill-set, and extensive experience. But once they retire, more often than not, that knowledge and those skills are lost. We do not put enough value on the more experienced members of our society, even though they are a key to moving sustainability forwards today.

Business schools will include a short programme specifically aimed at individuals who are thinking of retiring or have already retired. These students would have access to a set of courses that are specifically focused on the questions and concerns that this group of students has, but they would also have access to everything else happening on campus, including campus events, clubs and electives. In this way, in addition to preparing themselves for this new phase of their life, these students would also be actively contributing to the education and knowledge sharing that is happening on campus, with the other students, with faculty, with staff and with the community.

Idea 55. Global MBA

Sustainability leaders need to have a global view, to enable them to understand and work across countries and cultures around the world. Regardless of whether a graduate spends an entire career working in the local community or working across countries, having a better understanding of what differentiates and unites us will strengthen their abilities to lead and manage.

Rather than be based at one school in one city, business programmes will take place across several locations around the world. This will go much further and deeper than the traditional exchange programme. Students will start in one location and regularly throughout the degree will move to a different city around the world. By the end of the degree, they will have spent time on all continents, or if desired can focus in on a particular region of the world (e.g. Asia or Europe) or even move around a particular country (e.g. the different provinces of Canada). In each location, students will take a range of core and additional courses as well as completing projects that will introduce them to the business, cultural and sustainability realities in that region.

Idea 56. A series of experiences

Business programmes will not be made up of a series of classes as they are today. Instead, in order to graduate with a business degree, students will be required to complete a series of projects, some of short duration and others longer. Each project will focus on developing a particular set of skills, giving them first-hand experience and the ability to work in a variety of different situations. Each project will also relate to a particular challenge faced by local, national, regional and international organizations, businesses or communities.

Firstly, the students would take a range of projects in which they have a different responsibility in each. This could include being the lead for one project and finding other students to work with them, as well as working on someone else's team.

The projects would have to be completed with a range of different stakeholder groups, including government, NGOs, international organizations and various types of business – small, large, local or international. This will give students a better understanding of the different stakeholders that influence and are affected by the business sector. Where possible, they will also take place in different locations around the world.

Lastly, projects would focus on a variety of different themes. In one example, the student would need to start a new business and/or create a new product or service. In other projects they would work in teams that already exist and are ongoing. The projects would be based on real challenges that individual businesses, the business sector as a whole or even the international community are facing. Sample challenges could include developing an alternative to GDP, creating a new product or developing a campaign to change an unsustainable behaviour in a particular community.

In order to support students during these projects, faculty would act as advisors and would be available to help students with the development of the different skills they need to help complete their projects, whether these are in finance, team management or communication. There would be regularly scheduled short workshops on different topics to help prepare students who are about to start new projects or are interested in developing certain skills. The objective is to help students to apply what they learn through one experience to other, sometimes radically different, scenarios.

Students would be marked based on the work they do on their projects, how they are completed, reviews from their peers, and their ability to learn, take risks and adapt. Students would graduate once they have completed the full set of projects (within a predetermined time period). By the time students have completed the list of required projects, they should have all the skills necessary, and a lot of first-hand experience, to work in any organization. In that time they will have also made some interesting and meaningful contributions to their communities.

Idea 57. The mini-MBA

 The skills taught in an MBA are ones that are important to anyone's career. Whether you have trained as a doctor, an engineer, an artist or an athlete, these skills can be extremely useful.

With this in mind, the future MBA may no longer be a one- or two-year programme but rather a shorter programme that is done at the end of other Master's degree programmes. Once students finish a Master's-level studies in Economics, English Literature or Architecture, for example, they would then have access to a short, interdisciplinary MBA programme where they learn the business, leadership, entrepreneurship and, of course, sustainability-related skills that they can then apply in their respective fields. In this way, all graduates will be better prepared to make meaningful contributions to their respective disciplines and as managers going into the business sector will have a variety of specialized backgrounds that will be of use in the increasingly connected business environment.

Idea 58. The lifelong MBA

 The MBA is a moment in time. After graduation, alumni go through various subsequent phases in their career, phases where they could once again use the lessons and support that a business degree provides.

The future MBA will be a three- to four (plus)-year programme spread out over a lifetime. It begins some time after you have some work experience. Students would spend the first one or two years on campus completing a range of core courses and electives.

The remaining years would then be used throughout the student's lifetime. There would be a special course available for students who are considering retiring or have just retired to assist them in planning out their next steps. Another course would be available to parents who are thinking of going back to work either part- or full-time after or while raising children. A section would be open to alumni who are thinking of starting a business or who are working independently. There would be a range of courses of interest to individuals at different points of their career: managers, CEOs, board members, as well as on specific topics of interest and relevance to the business world today. Not only would this provide a more structured life-long learning experience but also the opportunity to connect and learn from individuals of all ages and at different stages of their life and career on campus and in the classroom.

6 The school

"Practise what you preach" is a commonly used phrase, but one that many business schools don't take seriously enough. In the future, business schools will explore sustainability within their own operations, both environmentally and socially, in more comprehensive and strategic ways, providing multiple opportunities for students, staff and faculty to engage in the process while pushing the boundaries of what is possible.

Idea 59. The new COO

Business schools are so busy working on day-to-day issues that often there are not enough opportunities to stand back and look at the bigger picture. How can business schools ensure that they take advantage of, and respond to, opportunities and challenges presented by the outside business and non-business world around sustainability?

The business school Chief Operating Officer (COO) will become a Chief Opportunity Officer. This person will be responsible for exploring opportunities both within and outside of the school. They will have a strong understanding of the work different faculty and researchers are doing on campus as well as the community, and the entrepreneurial and business environment surrounding the school, to be able to make connections between these groups that will strengthen the school as a whole. Chief Opportunity Officers will work to identify and facilitate cross-disciplinary opportunities and operate across the silos that exist within business schools to be able to explore ways for the school to learn, change, evolve and adapt to the world around them.

Idea 60. Making sure everyone is fed ... well

There are a lot of ways that universities are bringing more sustainable and local food onto campus. Farmers' markets on campus are increasingly popular, as is the provision of fair-trade and organic options. But how could you take this a step further?

In the future, food on campus will be provided by a series of short-term pop-up caterers or businesses. These businesses would provide everything including the coffee, catering for meetings, and lunch service. They could be established businesses or startups by chefs or other individuals. The focus would be on local and sustainable cuisine and ingredients. Groups selected would have a chance to test new ideas as well as get feedback from the student body. In return, the student body would get access to high quality, diverse and constantly changing sustainable food offerings.

Several different businesses operate within a business school besides food, including cleaning and transportation. Using the business school environment to test out, strengthen and support local businesses and entrepreneurs would, in turn, create a richer living and learning environment for all on campus.

Idea 61. Closed-loop campus

 Businesses will increasingly be closed-loop. They will manage the entire life-cycle of their products in a sustainable way, from the design to manufacturing and all the way to the end of life. At this stage, all waste will either be recaptured and reused or recycled endlessly into new products or biodegrade.

Business schools will also operate as closed-loop systems and their campus will generate no waste. Beyond extensive efforts to minimize waste in the first place, all waste relating to operations will be designed to be recaptured and then reused or composted. Systems will be put in place to sell certain waste streams to other organizations or to be able to trade, swap, barter, lend to, gift or share items with others on campus or part of the school community. Students and staff will be actively engaged in exploring opportunities to further develop and improve on these systems every year.

Idea 62. Campus harvest

 Business school campuses are often beautifully landscaped with a range of (hopefully native) plants and flowers. But what if the campus land was also used as an opportunity to teach, engage and feed the university community?

The business school campus will be planted with native fruit trees and other edible plants. Yearly harvest time will be a festival that sees students, staff and alumni come back to campus to pick the fruits. All produce will be used on campus or sold at local markets, creating a fund to help support the management of the campus farm. All that is harvested will be used; over-ripened fruit may be used to create jams and other products. Waste will be turned into compost and used on campus or sold. The campus may also have beehives, not only providing for the pollination of plants on campus, but also offering a regular supply of high-quality honey to be sold or used as school gifts for visitors. Some schools may take this even further by using outdoor common areas for grazing animals or for planting crops. Designated areas, even rooftops, will be divided into small plots that students and staff can use for one or several school terms to try their hand at planting vegetables and herbs, and which in turn provide a relaxing distraction.

Idea 63. No energy needed

University campuses are complex environments that require a large amount of energy for lighting, computers, technology, air conditioning and heating. In the future, business schools will become energy self-sufficient. They will not only generate enough energy for their own needs on campus, but will also be able to support other businesses located nearby.

Schools will continue to become more energy-efficient by minimizing energy use and through the use of leading-edge technologies. In order to support their energy needs at this point, they will tap into a range of renewable energy options. Depending on the location of the business school, these will include, but of course are not limited to, wind, solar or geothermal, with some produced on-campus. Flooring across campus will collect the kinetic energy of students and staff walking, running and climbing stairs. The use of gym equipment, such as stationary bikes, will help to generate power to run the gym or collect energy for the cafeteria. Students and staff will be actively engaged in exploring possible options and putting them into practice.

Idea 64. At your fingertips

University campuses are increasingly putting significant effort into becoming more sustainable businesses themselves, in particular in relation to their own operations. For many, the goal is to create more environmentally sustainable, self-sufficient and efficient campuses.

In order for a business school to know exactly what is happening at any given moment on campus relating to energy and water use, waste generation or progress on any environmental goals set within the school, students and staff will have access to an online platform that is prominently displayed on campus. The platform would present a wide range of real-time data: for example, how many cars and bikes are on campus at any given moment or how many windows are open while the air conditioner is running. This would increase students' and staff's awareness of their immediate environment and impact upon it, and allow them to see problem areas, react and make changes in real time, or just keep up the good work.

Idea 65. The ideal workplace

 What makes a business a place people want to work, a place where employees will give their best, day in and day out, a business where employees love what they do and tell others? What if, in the future, it were business schools that regularly won the "Best Place to Work" awards?

Considering how many faculty do research on employee engagement and efficiency, what if these learnings were applied to their own places of business?

Business schools could be a space to test out how to be the ideal workplace, one where quotas are no longer necessary, equal pay and opportunity are the norm, people work smarter and are more engaged, and the schools are better off because of it. They could be a place in which to create an environment where employees have the space to think about the impacts of their decisions and make better decisions because of that. The additional bonus: this provides a live case study for students about what is possible for them to bring into their own workplaces in the future.

Idea 66. Living

How do you facilitate connections between different students from a variety of disciplines beyond what is happening during classes?

Business schools will have a special residence where students can live. The building will be self-sufficient and use all the latest green building technologies, including small community gardens at the ground level and on the roof. A variety of living accommodation types will be available, ranging from dorm style to more private suites for singles, couples or even families. The rooms will be organized in a way that will allow the spaces to be reconfigured and shifted based on changing circumstances. The residents would be students as well as a handful of recent alumni and would be a mix of both business students as well as students from other non-business disciplines. Throughout the residence one would find a range of large common areas set up to encourage the sharing of ideas and collaboration on projects. There would be a resource space with access to advisors 24 hours a day to encourage such collaboration.

Idea 67. Engaging as shareholders

Universities hold billions of dollars in corporate stock. As shareholders, they have the opportunity and the responsibility to positively impact those companies and influence their sustainability policies and strategies. How do we turn universities from passive to active investors for the benefit of the universities, the companies and society as a whole?

Future business students will engage with faculty and staff at the business school to examine the companies the university has shares in, and how they choose which shares to invest in or divest from. They will explore opportunities to vote on different issues, attend annual meetings, and put forth or comment on shareholder resolutions relating to social and environmental topics. They will also collaborate with other universities and shareholders to influence corporate policies.

If business schools are going to continue to put an emphasis on shareholders in their teachings, then they should also prepare students to be the kind of active shareholder that a more sustainable business sector needs.

Idea 68. Reporting

 Leading businesses are pushing the boundaries of what is possible in corporate reporting. They are increasing disclosure, becoming more transparent and reporting on the issues that are most material to their businesses. They are experimenting with environmental profit-and-loss statements, integrated reporting and other formats that will likely become the norm for a more comprehensive way of communicating their progress in the future.

Instead of lagging behind business, business schools will be ahead of the game when it comes to reporting. They will be creating, shaping and testing out innovative new ways of reporting which will inspire the way that other organizations, such as businesses and NGOs, report on their activities, both in terms of quantitative and qualitative data. Business schools will develop a form of reporting that is perfectly adapted to their unique environment, that will provide a more transparent and engaging picture of the institution, its goals and targets, its successes and challenges, its impact and relationships, and its effectiveness at doing what it says it does. Annual reports will take on different shapes, shifting information off the printed page and bringing it to life through online platforms, events and other projects with lessons and insights shared with the wider community. The whole university community, including students, staff and faculty, will be actively engaged in the annual reporting process.

Idea 69. Practise what you teach

 In the future, business schools will manage and run one or a small number of specialized businesses on or nearby campus. Students would be actively engaged in running these already existing businesses and embedding sustainability concepts throughout their operations. A marketing student could be responsible for developing and implementing a new marketing plan for the business. An accounting student would be responsible for managing the books around more integrated reporting. Schools could choose to develop business opportunities based on their unique surroundings and this in itself could help differentiate themselves from other schools. For example, a business school based in a location ideal for grape growing could create its own wine/tourism business that in turn would attract students interested in related industries.

Idea 70. The little things

There are many big things that could be done to strengthen management education in ways that prepare graduates to be sustainability champions. But just as important, if not more so, are the little things. These details can strengthen or completely undermine whatever strategy you have in place or message you want to communicate. The little things are part of a culture that can enhance or detract from the school's mission.

In the future, business schools will need to pay more attention to the little things. What you say to students during the first weeks of school, what you give to your students or guests as gifts, the words you use in communications with students, who you invite to speak, what kind of behaviour is acceptable/unacceptable, all send strong signals as to what is and is not important.

Take the little details seriously – they often have the biggest impact.

7 The system

Business school programmes around the world are surprisingly similar in the way they operate as well as what they teach. They are also all affected by a larger system that often does more to reinforce the status quo than to support and encourage change. In the future, the sector will go beyond just identifying these challenges, to taking control and creating a system that supports and facilitates these necessary changes.

Idea 71. Easily accessible

 Although many consider that teaching is the key role of business schools, one could argue that in practice it is secondary to research. A significant and increasing amount of resources go into faculty research. Faculty are selected and rewarded based on their research performance, with the primary means of assessment being their publication record, publications that are widely aimed at an academic audience. The challenge is not only that many of the publications in this space are not readily accessible to business practitioners, but that they are often not written in a way that is useful or relevant to the actual challenges that business is dealing with.

In the future, faculty research, as well as the systems that reward that research, will be connected in a much stronger way to what is relevant to the business sector. The kind of research, the way research is conducted, where it is published, the format in which it is published and the way success is measured will change to make it more impactful and more collaborative. Faculty will be required, and able, to translate and communicate these findings in ways that are usable by those communities who could best benefit from this new knowledge. They will publish research results on a wide variety of platforms including blogs that are free of charge and easily accessible, and will receive instantaneous feedback. Research value may even be judged by users over time.

Idea 72. Ranking value

When it comes to choosing a business degree programme, and in particular an MBA, rankings rule. But what do these rankings really tell you about a school? They may say a lot about how you will be viewed post-graduation for future jobs, etc., but do they really say anything about the quality of the education that you will receive or the position a particular educational institution holds in society? How do we create a ranking that rewards creativity, transformation, and the ability to prepare future leaders rather than the continuation of the status quo or post business school salary?

In the future, business school rankings will be generated based on very different, more relevant, measures. For example, rankings could be based on the value that a particular business school provides to society. This value will be determined based on research, community engagement, quality of education and training programmes, among other things. The measure of value will not be solely a quantitative one, so, for example, more research published in perceived leading journals will not necessarily give you a better ranking. It will be based on the value of that research, as well as the contribution of a school's graduates to society in the short, medium and long term. Rankings could be based on the capabilities developed in graduates of the school and their ability to successfully use these. Programme fees might even become tied to these "rankings" or scores, fluctuating from year to year. Students (recent and long-time graduates), peers, business partners and the community will be involved in generating the different values for this ranking.

Idea 73. Rethinking the doctorate

In the same way that we must strengthen business degrees to be able to create the next generation of sustainable managers and leaders that the world needs, even more important perhaps is the necessity to strengthen the doctoral programmes that create the next generation of professors and researchers that teach these students and support business schools.

The current system is heavily weighted towards training doctoral students to publish rather than towards developing their teaching skills. In the future, these students will have more opportunities to pursue different paths. Students as well as academics will have the opportunity to either specialize in research or in teaching, or a combination of the two. Both tracks will have incentives for promotion and career development and, based on their choice of track, students will receive additional training at the beginning and throughout their careers. This training could include placements within organizations focused on the topic of their research, or teaching training. There will be more interdisciplinary options, partnership with industry, and online models that enable working professionals to pursue new ideas with leading scholars.

If we change the next generation of doctoral graduates to create better teachers, facilitators and researchers, perhaps they can in turn tackle the challenges that are limiting our ability to really move forward in many ways. This in itself may require another 100 ideas.

Idea 74. Accreditation

A significant amount of resources are put into gaining and retaining accreditation for a business degree. This seal of approval is important, sometimes necessary. However, not only are these resources perhaps better placed elsewhere but the accreditation process ends up guiding a lot of the decisions that a particular school is making in terms of its curriculum, its operations, and its choice of faculty—which serves to entrench the status quo. Can any of these 100 ideas be implemented without a change in the accreditation system?

In the future, accreditation systems will become more adaptable and flexible to different approaches in business schools, providing much more space and support for schools to experiment and explore alternative directions, in particular in terms of curriculum and research. Accreditation will likely cease to exist in the way it is today and instead reinvent itself by becoming a giant global think-tank exploring and testing ideas. Accreditation will strengthen the incentives and resources to enable changes to happen based on the needs of business, students, society and the schools themselves.

Idea 75. A web of learning

Case studies are at the core of many business schools, not just as a publishing opportunity for faculty, but also as a primary teaching tool for students. However, not only are they based on past events, but more often than not they significantly oversimplify issues that occur in business and so provide very limited, if any, space or time to see a challenge within the wider context of the business itself and society at large. Each is usually a single moment in time.

The case study of the future will become much more dynamic and connected. Businesses will regularly create a range of live case studies based on the development of the current challenges that they are facing. These cases will be coordinated with faculty and will be available to all business schools around the world. Case studies will connect and build on previous case studies, and provide opportunities to think ahead into the future. They will connect with cases that demonstrate the impacts of decisions made in the past and highlight the impacts on social and environmental issues. Students may have the opportunity to study the cases in the classroom or move to relevant locations locally or even internationally to better experience the case. They will create a web of information exploring in more depth what is happening in the business world.

Students will have the space to develop their recommendations in a number of ways, using live information. And, rather than having a right or wrong answer, solutions will be brought together from students from across the world, providing different perspectives on an issue or challenge. The subjects of the case studies themselves will also have access to this feedback.

Idea 76. Empowering recruiters

 Let's assume that the business school of the future becomes a reality. Schools start creating graduates with the potential to be true leaders in the jobs that they choose and the communities in which they live. But ultimately, if they aren't hired, if a company cannot see that potential, then it becomes a hard sell to potential students. It is one thing for business schools to

develop capable, future-oriented leaders, but it is another thing for recruiters to identify, seek out and build capacity that places a value on this.

Recruiters will be actively engaged in the business schools of the future beyond just company presentation and recruiting. Within the businesses they represent, they will be more knowledgeable and aware of multiple, unique potential employee profiles. They will act as a stronger connection between the business and the school over the full school year, taking a bigger interest in the way that their possible recruits are trained and how they develop over the programme. Recruiting will no longer be a process that takes up a significant amount of time and effort from students throughout their programme, allowing them to focus on getting the most out of their degree. Instead, recruiters will adapt and follow the degree, becoming part of conversations when it is most appropriate for the students and school.

Idea 77. How am I doing?

 Increasingly, the way that we evaluate the performance of employees will change. This trend will carry over, or perhaps start, in business schools. A grade at the end of a long course, be that an A, B, C or D, says little about what students learnt and, more importantly, how they learnt it and their ability to use or even recall that information after graduation.

Business schools will experiment with a range of ways to help students understand how they are progressing through the degree. Different courses will have different kinds of "grading" mechanisms. A student could receive multiple grades per course based on performance, competencies, understanding, and ability to apply the information. Students could even grade themselves. Business schools may very well not have any grades or even require grades to access a particular programme. Instead, evaluations will be more like performance reviews, combining both a faculty's perspective as well as perspectives from peers and from the students themselves.

Idea 78. Peer-to-peer lending

 An MBA is an expensive degree, especially when you add living expenses and, for international students, often higher programme fees too. This undoubtedly prohibits many prospective students from beginning one. Graduates usually end up with higher salaries when they're finished. But not all students benefit from this and the post MBA debt often forces students to choose certain jobs over others and filters the kind of students that apply in the first place. How can an MBA be made accessible to a wider range of potential students with a more diverse set of post-graduation plans?

There are a growing number of platforms online that facilitate peer-to-peer lending – usually one individual lending or giving another individual money, often to start or expand a business idea. Students enrolled in the future MBA could have the possibility of having their programme fees partially or completely funded through small loans or scholarships provided by alumni or family and friends. A similar platform could also allow alumni and businesses to provide micro-scholarships to students with backgrounds or goals they want to support.

Idea 79. Admissions boot camp

The challenge presented by providing one type of testing to enter into a business programme is that you inevitably attract a certain kind of person who is able to perform well in that test. How can business schools more successfully attract a wider range of students into their programme who could be valuable additions to the business school community and successful alumni?

Business schools in future will no longer require a quantitative/qualitative test to gain entry as they widely do today. Instead, they will explore a range of ways to gain admission into the programme. Students have the chance to go through one or several activities to raise their chances of entry depending on their educational and career background. One example could be the "Admissions Boot Camp". At the Admissions Boot Camp potential students would come to campus for a long weekend or two during or before their admission process where they would be introduced to a range of basic business skills they will need to successfully complete the MBA and be put through some individual and group exercises, both in person and virtually. Not only will this allow the school to assess their suitability, it will also give potential students a chance to learn more about the school and make an impression with the admissions officers.

Idea 80. An MBA tax

If the future MBA is a programme where students are trained and prepared to be the sustainable leaders that organizations and the world needs today and tomorrow, they will play a crucial role in society. If this is the case, society as a whole may be able to help cover some, or all, of the costs of such a programme.

Business school programme fees could be paid for by using money collected through a range of taxes from companies aimed at strengthening the sustainability environment for the business sector. These funds could even come from penalties and fees paid by companies who have not complied with sustainability laws and regulations. Funds coming from different penalties could go to funding programmes and research within business schools relating to those specific topics. For example, a fund made up of money collected from penalties related to emissions could fund climate change research and energy courses and programmes within the business school programme, providing a range of project work for students, and faculty, to dive into.

8 The community

Business schools often operate in a bubble, physically located in a community yet without any significant interaction with it. In the future, business schools will be a much more integral part of their surrounding community, engaging in a wide range of community activities. Students and staff will work on projects that strengthen local organizations, government and businesses and vice versa. At the same time, multiple opportunities will exist for organizations and individuals from the community to participate in projects, businesses, research and other activities happening within the business school, turning it into a hub of multidisciplinary, sustainable business thinking and acting.

Idea 81. Business school pop-ups

 Communities are filled with empty retail spaces. The pop-up retail movement invites individuals and brands, both well known and yet to be discovered, to use these spaces for short periods of time to test out new ideas, sell their products and share their message. They also inject energy into a community.

Business schools will have their own pop-up business space, either in a building managed by the school or in a range of spaces in the community to which the school has access. These spaces would be open to business-school-related pop-ups, and would be used from anywhere between an hour to several days by faculty, staff, students and alumni to test out new ideas, give a short course, sell new products or share insights on topics of interest. Most importantly, it will give students and staff an opportunity to interact with their local community in a tangible way.

The schools themselves will also arrange a similar space on campus for members of the community to come in and interact directly with students and staff in the same way.

Idea 82. The cooperative

 There are a growing number of different business models that put sustainability at their core. Could business schools, which currently often operate as something between an educational institution and a traditional business, be organized using a model that would enable them to accomplish their aims better while contributing more to society?

A cooperative is a business enterprise owned and controlled by the very members that it serves. Cooperatives put people before profit by helping their members achieve their shared social, cultural and economic aspirations.

Business schools could become cooperatives with students and staff – future, present and past – making up its membership base. They would focus on helping their members to achieve their educational and life goals as well as contributing to the knowledge base in their communities and internationally. They would provide a range of different services to meet their members' needs and take a long-term view, exploring new ideas and opportunities. As their governance would be based on balanced democratic control, they would hold themselves accountable for limiting negative impacts that might otherwise be overlooked.

Idea 83. Beyond business

Business schools will have short courses that introduce students to a range of parallel careers they could have during their lives, and provide them with the necessary skills to succeed in those areas. This would enable graduates to have a wider impact across society. One module would focus on engagement in politics. This non-partisan, issue-neutral course will focus on how to run a campaign, including budgeting, polling, fundraising, public speaking, staffing, working with consultants, and other topics. Students will also have the chance to work on real campaigns or even start their own. Another module would be focused on being a board member for either a company or a not-for-profit. All the courses would be accessible to alumni.

Idea 84. Adopt-a-business

 A business school campus sits within a community filled with small business owners. These small business owners may cater to the university community, or want to cater to them; however, they may also be just starting or struggling to make ends meet. They are experiencing, in real time, the challenges that students will be learning about in the classroom just next door. But the connections between universities and businesses and other organizations in their immediate community are often weak or even non-existent.

Students will have the opportunity to be paired, in small groups or as individuals, with local businesses and organizations as well as local government projects. The businesses themselves, which could, for example, be the corner store, a local pub, an artist, a hotel, a day-care centre, a small business owner or a community group, would apply to be part of the programme. Students would have the chance to select businesses of interest to them and would spend some time within the business during the school year, learning more about how it operates, volunteering or working in the business, but also providing advice and help as and when needed. A series of events would also take place on campus to facilitate the interaction of the students with their and other students' adopted businesses.

Idea 85. Genius bar

Business schools around the world are home to some great minds – individuals who have spent their life studying a particular topic. They are very knowledgeable, but very few people get the opportunity to learn from these individuals unless they attend one of their classes, or read their book.

Business schools will provide a space where professors and subject matter experts would be available for short periods of time to meet with and answer the questions of any student, staff or other individual from the wider community. For the local community, this means the opportunity to interact and learn, from specialists to whom they don't normally have access, lessons that could help move their own projects forward; and for the professors it provides opportunities to explore the broader implications and reach of their work and research.

Idea 86. Change-makers in residence

In the future, the walls put up between business schools and the rest of the world will be small, or even non-existent. Plenty of opportunities will exist for business schools to interact in meaningful ways with the local community, and vice versa. A range of programmes will be put in place that invite individuals onto campus who have something to say or a question to ask, to do special projects, spending between one week and one year exploring a particular issue or a challenge in their business or in their community that they are looking to further explore and take action on.

Themes can also be established by the business school based on their focus areas, and individuals can apply to do projects that fit in with those themes. Each project will have an outcome, which will be presented to the school community and to the individual's own professional community that could result in more in-depth research, a prototype, or a plan of action. Rather than one or two such individuals, space could be given for dozens of change-makers to spend varying time in residence, taking from and contributing to the business school community, as a parallel programme to the traditional degrees. These "thinkers" could also be brought in to co-teach courses alongside academic staff.

Idea 87. Flagship store

More and more businesses are opening flagship stores where they invite the public to be part of their brand and to interact with it. Business schools, on the other hand, are often in locked buildings only accessible to students and staff.

In the future, business schools will have a storefront on campus or elsewhere in the city, and even in other cities around the world, where the school can interact with the community and bring their projects, research and ideas to life. This "store", staffed by students, staff, faculty, researchers, alumni and even business partners, would be a space for the public, local businesses, community groups and individuals to interact with the school and vice versa, to raise the profile of the business school and the work they do.

The store could have a variety of elements, including interactive information on programmes the school offers. It would have presentations of past, current and future research topics, in a format and language easily accessible to the general public, as well as providing opportunities for the wider community to get engaged in or use some of this research. Advisory services on sustainability topics would also be available.

A number of short courses open and accessible to all (both in terms of admission and pricing) would also be provided, exploring specific sustainability-related topics with a focus on providing updates and overviews of current issues.

Idea 88. City campus

Is the classroom the best place for students to learn about business? Although the classroom is an environment that allows students to focus on the topic at hand, it also separates them physically and emotionally from it, limiting the different ways students can learn and interact with a chosen topic.

Business school classes in the future will not happen on a campus in a traditional classroom. Instead, students will have many of their classes in different locations across the city. A course on social entrepreneurship would take place at a social entrepreneurship hub where entrepreneurs share office space and collaborate or in the offices of a social enterprise. A lecture on integrated reporting would happen in the offices of an association or business working on these topics. A class focused on responsible advertising in the food industry would take place in the aisles of a supermarket or at the headquarters of a leading company in responsible advertising. This would strengthen the lessons by putting them into a context that the students can experience and explore in real time.

Idea 89. Activating alumni

Business programmes typically accept the brightest minds into their programmes. Cohorts create new bonds that last a lifetime and shared traditions over time enable relationships to develop across generations. These alumni go on to create and work at some of the leading businesses around the world. How can a business school better capitalize on that energy and expertise, to connect alumni to become a powerful force for each other, together and with the wider community?

The business school alumni network of the future will facilitate connections between alumni on multiple levels. It will continue to enable alumni to search for each other and connect but will do so in a much more active way. If alumni are travelling or free between meetings, they will be able to connect with alumni who are physically close by, connections that could ultimately turn into new opportunities. If an alumnus is working on a new product or project, he or she can tap into a sub-set of alumni to help online or in person for impromptu brainstorming and feedback sessions. The alumni network becomes a support system for small or big projects on a day-to-day basis, providing a range of different viewpoints on topics that are being worked upon.

The school itself will also better capitalize on the energy and expertise of its alumni base to strengthen its own operations and offerings, crowdsourcing ideas for new courses, and harnessing its energy to bring about wider change in the business community.

9 The bigger picture

The business degree of the future will reflect more closely the realities of business today and tomorrow by putting a major focus on the bigger picture, all that business impacts, that impacts business and beyond, in both positive and less positive ways. Students will learn about different stakeholders including NGOs, government and the United Nations, and how to collaborate with them. They will engage in projects that help move social and environmental goals forward.

Idea 90. Collaborative action

The international community is regularly putting in place, and is actively working to reach, key goals and targets around various sustainability issues. For example, the current Sustainable Development Goals (SDGs) present an ambitious agenda for governments, business, and civil society worldwide. Few business students or faculty have heard of these but, due to their increasing influence over business practice, should be more widely discussed in business education.

Business schools of the future will be actively engaged in the work being done in the international and business community on development and sustainability issues. Research agendas will align with international priorities and real business challenges. These topics will not just come up in assignments, courses and readings but in consulting projects and partnerships, making business schools and their students and staff key partners in working with communities at local, national and international levels to reach these crucial goals.

Idea 91. Playing games

Individuals of all ages are spending time playing highly addictive video games. A growing number of these games aim to help solve bigger challenges, in particular in the sciences, using individual players to solve tiny bits of the problem and bringing all of these tiny solutions together into larger ones. The puzzle-focused game Foldit, played by hundreds of thousands of players, came up with a major AIDS breakthrough in a matter of just three weeks.

Students in business schools, as well as the public at large, will have the chance to develop and play collaborative video games which give them a chance, using real data, to build new businesses, explore solutions to business and sustainability challenges, and explore new business models that make more sense for the planet and society. They will give players a chance to explore what does, or really should, make up a successful business and business environment. The games will be open-source and researchers and students alike will be able to explore solutions through the game.

Idea 92. Global centres

 Each individual business school has a range of centres on campus that explore a particular topic through research projects and partnerships. Many business schools have very similar centres, in some cases doing very similar work and coming to very similar conclusions.

The academic community thrives on being able to have the flexibility to research what they want, in whatever way they want and when they want. They often do not focus enough on ensuring that what they work on is in a format that is useful to the business and global community. This results in an inefficient use of resources and, more importantly, missed opportunities.

In the future, centres will change from being managed locally on each campus/university to being connected across disciplines and industry sectors, globally. They will bring together leading experts from a range of fields, campuses and universities into one global or regional centre, ensuring maximum value and impact from their work. Their work will be built upon and extended by others.

Idea 93. Beyond events

 An important element of sustainability is that of eliminating waste and increasing efficiency. This isn't just physical waste, but wasted time and wasted opportunities. In order for the international community to move forward with sustainable development, all actors need to engage fully. Business schools have several key roles to play.

One way this can be achieved is through the organization of more impactful events. Although we all spend time attending and participating in events, few events effectively bring together new information, new experiences, new solutions, or generally have an impact in the fields they bring people together to discuss.

In the future, the way that business schools convene and deliver events and conferences will change. Educational institutions will bring people together to share, discuss, network and learn, and they will also create a safe environment where stakeholders can meet to move specific discussions forward, exploring and putting in place concrete plans of action and reporting on their progress. This will provide countless benefits to the school itself, the students in terms of learning opportunities, faculty in terms of research opportunities and the international community more generally.

Idea 94. A sustainability test lab

A number of businesses have internal departments that focus on testing out new sustainability ideas. Ideas that work then get embedded across other parts of the business. Ideas that don't work become opportunities to learn lessons that can be applied to future projects. Many innovative products and services have come from these types of departments.

Business schools are in an ideal position to implement similar test labs that bring together expert faculty, students, alumni and representatives from the community to explore current and future sustainability challenges and test out new ideas in a safe and creative environment.

The test lab of the future business school will not only explore sustainability challenges faced by the local, international and business community, but also sustainability challenges on campus. It would be a space to explore the development of new courses, revisiting existing courses or to start new campus greening projects. Successes and lessons learnt here could be applied and shared across the school and the wider community.

Idea 95. Environment

Economics already enjoys a prominent position in all business school curriculums. It sets the scene within which business stories take place. But this only tells part of the story. Sustainability goes beyond economics to consider the social and natural environment as well. These three areas will be the basis of courses that form a key part of the business school curriculum of the future.

Having a basic understanding of how the natural environment works is important for business students. These represent not just resources used by companies but issues material to all. The Natural Environment module would provide a brief overview, from a business perspective, of planet earth, how our natural environment affects our daily lives and the way we work today and in the future. Topics covered will include an introduction to biodiversity, climate, ecosystems, water and how the world's systems are all connected. It will also explore the impact that humans are having on the planet, both positive and negative, and the range of international goals, targets and organizations working to strengthen and protect the natural environment at the local, national, regional and international levels.

Idea 96. Society

 Delivered in parallel to the above course on Environment, the course on the Social Environment will look at the impact of the 7 billion humans on earth, where they are and what they are doing. This includes population and demographics, indigenous people, language and religion, and tangible and intangible culture. It will look at the impact of humans on earth, including buildings, urbanization and transportation. International development could be explored more broadly as well as the social challenges the world is facing and what needs to be/is being done about them. The course will also introduce students to the range of international goals, targets and organizations working to strengthen and protect our social environment at the local, national, regional and international levels, and learn why this is relevant for business.

Idea 97. From shareholders to stakeholders

 "Stakeholder" is not a word that often comes up in a business degree. But, because graduates will find it increasingly hard to work for a business that operates in isolation from the world around it, it is important that students understand its meaning.

On the one hand, students need to be able to recognize, understand and be accountable to their business stakeholders: those groups that are directly or indirectly affected by the business. This goes beyond just shareholders and investors to include, for example, employees and their families, customers, the media, local community groups, and supplier companies.

There is another key group of stakeholders. During the first Earth Summit in 1992, which brought together leaders of governments from around the world to discuss sustainable development (many subsequent events have taken place since then), nine major stakeholders (also known as the Major Groups) were identified and, to this day, are still consulted in meetings of the United Nations. These are Children and Youth, Farmers, Indigenous Peoples, Women, Local Authorities, Workers and Trade Unions, NGOs and the Scientific and Technological Community. The ninth group is Business and Industry. These are the world's shareholders and they each have a say in how we move forward. By the end of their degrees, graduates will be able to identify, communicate and collaborate with these different groups.

Idea 98. Collaborative solutions

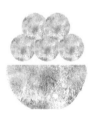

What if every time a student was learning about a challenge they were, at the same time, also helping to solve that challenge? Whether it is environmental, social, or related to the new SDGs, each challenge can be divided into thousands of individual challenges that need solutions, fresh ideas and action.

Business schools will play a key role in providing these solutions. Individual schools and groups of schools will be invited to address one or a range of key questions that are being tackled by the international community. Class discussions and assignments, projects, case competitions, research and events will all become focused on exploring possible answers to these specific questions.

Students will be able to connect their research topics and projects to these challenges, exploring new aspects or taking an existing proposed solution and building on to it, adding to the global database of knowledge that could help move key sustainability issues forward for both the business and world community. The result would be a global map of information, accessible and usable by all, which connects the work done by millions of students and researchers globally.

Idea 99. A change in language

"Saving the world", "doing good", "green", "sustainability": these words inspire and encourage. But, equally, they separate and distinguish, and for many students "sustainability" and "business" are two completely different concepts. Many of these new sustainability-focused electives and courses are preaching to the converted. But what about those students, perhaps the vast majority, who are not yet convinced?

Without using a separate word or term such as "sustainability", we cannot necessarily have the focused conversations that are needed, or ensure that the conversations are being had at all. But the vast number of the words used in this space do not begin to convey the number of very concrete ideas, tools, concepts and realities that they encompass. "Sustainability" risks being perceived as something different from mainstream business: an addition, perhaps a nice-to-have, but not universally relevant or accessible. Is it philanthropy? Is it volunteering in the community? Is it recycling bins? Or is it really about using sustainability as a tool to strengthen and innovate business and deal with challenges and opportunities that affect us all?

In the future, these discussions will be seen not as trends, or nice-to-haves, or topics students love to engage in. Rather, they will be seen as core business topics that encompass all business disciplines and intertwine between them. The language we use to judge the success of a business will change significantly to encompass social and environmental factors more fully. The two meanings for the word "sustainability", both in terms of triple bottom line and in terms of long-term profitability, will mean the same in all students' eyes.

Idea 100. Tomorrow

 What will the future company, the future NGO, the future consumer, the future customer, even the future business degree look like? Individuals and companies make a lot of money predicting the answers to these unpredictable questions. The reality is that it will be the next generation of managers and leaders who will ultimately determine and work in these future organizations. Could they be more actively engaged in, right from the start, not only exploring what that future might look like, but also helping to shape it?

In a class called "Tomorrow", students will come together to determine and debate how our actions today impact society in the future. In a series of ongoing discussions over the course of their programme, classes of students will become futurists, tapping into their diverse experience and backgrounds to explore and predict global trends, scenarios and opportunities they believe will become new business realities throughout their careers. These exercises will encourage students to think about what kind of future they would like, a future that will work for the planet and society as well as for the business sector. It will also focus on the now and how they can shape and reach the desired future through the work they do post-graduation through their career choices and business decisions. Graduates will play a much more active role in taking responsibility for that future and recognizing the power they have to ultimately shape and change it.

50 Questions

So how would you create the business school of the future? The Future MBA project is one of idea generation and then taking those ideas, exploring them, testing and implementing them. Here are 50 question to help you generate your own unique possibilities.

1. How do we prepare students to respond and react to new information as it arises?
2. How long should a business degree last?
3. How can business schools interact with the community in meaningful and innovative ways?
4. How do we engage business schools in current sustainability goals, challenges and targets?
5. How do we build in more time and opportunities for reflection?
6. What are the most important lessons of a business degree?
7. How do we empower graduates throughout their careers not just to work in the current system but also to bring about positive change?

8. How do we encourage innovative thinking and the development of new ideas across the school and beyond?

9. How do we organize the classroom to encourage more effective learning and interaction?

10. How do we encourage stronger connections across the university? And across business schools?

11. How can business schools better capitalize on the energy and expertise of their alumni?

12. Are centres as effective as they could be? How could they be rethought?

13. How do you create graduates with a multidisciplinary point of view?

14. How do we create better tools to facilitate learning?

15. How should/can technology be used in the classroom/ degree?

16. How can we create a network of business schools that are globally able to take action on and move sustainability forward?

17. How do you expose students to different ways of thinking and different perspectives on the issues they are interested in/learning?

18. How do we create a ranking that rewards creativity, impact and the ability to prepare leaders? Should we have rankings at all? What should they value?

19. How can we make business degrees more accessible to a wider range of students with a broader range of career aspirations and also at different points in their lives/ careers?

20. How can we prepare students to be better collaborators and not just competitors?

21. How can we create a truly sustainable campus?

22. How do we share faculty expertise/research with a wider audience?

23. How do we make business schools the ideal place to work?

24. What does a leader look like? What should a leader look like? What kind of leader do you want to be?

25. How much should an MBA really cost?

26. Should business schools have a dress code?

27. How can we create stronger courses that have an impact on students and beyond?

28. How can we ensure that faculty research plays a key role in moving global sustainability goals forward?

29. What does, or should, work–life balance look like? What would that look like in a business school?

30. What should the purpose of a business degree be? For students? For society? For business?

31. Should every discipline and degree programme have a business component?

32. Is how to start a business a key skill that all students should not only learn, but practise?

33. How do we train the next generation of faculty? What should the doctorate programme look like?

34. How do we measure impact?

35. What little things make a big impact in business schools when it comes to sustainability?

36. What other, non-business knowledge and skills would be important for students to gain to be better managers?

37. How could a business degree actively facilitate more learning from fellow students?

38. Can an MBA be like a one-of-a-kind, tailor-made suit?

39. Do classes need to take place in classrooms? Where else?

40. How do we expose students to different business environments and cultures from around the world without leaving the classroom?

41. How do we make business schools more accountable? To whom?

42. How can we tap into the power of crowds to create more sustainable business schools and programmes?

43. Who owns/manages/is responsible for the business school?

44. What is the role of the business school within society?

45. What kind of underlying culture should be promoted through MBAs?

46. Should business degrees be focused on shareholders or stakeholders?

47. Should business schools exist at all?

48. How do students/faculty communicate their progress/abilities/successes?

49. What would your ideal business school look like? What would you change? Take away? Add?

50. What questions would you ask?

Index: The 100 Ideas

6. The school 71

7. The system. 81